BROTHER HAROLD AND ROGER:

Spirit and Channel, Year One, 300+ Patients

BY ROGER A. LYONS

TABLE OF CONTENTS

PREFACE

I was born in 1948 and grew up in New York City during the post-World War II era.

The first thing I consciously remember was when I was five years old and in my bed late one night, searching for sleep. I laid there watching headlights appear and disappear from the ceiling in the bedroom and I remember that my first thoughts were based in fear because I did not know what caused these lights. I do specifically remember my decision to accept these lights as real and not dangerous to me, as my mother had suggested. My first experience with trust paid off in large dividends!

Growing up, I was closer to my mother than my father. Several years later, I calculated that my father was 52 years old when I was born, and my mother was twenty years younger, in her early thirties. This vast age difference between my father and me, better than anything else, probably explains our lack of closeness.

My maternal grandmother was also a very important presence for me as I grew up. My mother and grandmother were very close, and as a result, I became quite attached to both of them. My grandmother was born and raised in England, and in the early 1900's, moved to the United States with her husband after the birth of their first son. After they relocated, my grandfather began a career as a chemist with a paper business located in West Virginia.

As a child, my grandmother would carefully talk to me about other people and spoke about what thoughts she felt were jogging through their minds. While this was couched as a "game", it was definitely a use of her intuitive talents in a knowing way. Any time we were near a group of people, whether in the park or a restaurant, she would look around and pick out one or more people. She would then talk to me about what they were thinking, planning, or doing.

This became a natural way of life for me as we discussed such matters openly and normally. In her own way, she helped to create an intuitive person who learned how to "read" people very well. This ultimately developed into keenly perceptive skills which became very valuable to me during my sales career. Later in life, these perceptive and intuitive skills proved invaluable as I communicated with the spirit world and with my current work with Brother Harold. My grandmother can easily be credited for helping me develop my abilities and guiding me, which eventually would lead me to Brother Harold.

I remember in college those times my mother would telephone, and occasionally started conversations by asking me what was on my mind. She always knew if I had a problem, and my concerns often spilled out of me quickly.

Years later, my grandmother and grandfather (divorced after fifty years of marriage) lived in cities hundreds of miles apart. At that time, they did not communicate with each other. In what proved to be an unusual scenario, they both died at the same minute of the same day. My mother received two telephone calls bearing the same sad news within five minutes of each other. An unusual event, which was followed by a double funeral for them held in Virginia.

Two years after my college graduation, I was typing a letter in my home office one afternoon when I "knew" that my grandmother was standing behind me even though she had passed away three years earlier. The hair on the back of my neck stood on end as I turned in my chair to see her.

Unfortunately, I could not visually "see" her although I knew she was there. Feeling slightly panicked, I immediately left the house and drove around for an hour, mulling this unlikely event over. Now, I wish I had been more accepting of her appearance. I remember telling my mother about this and her response. She assured me that my grandmother would never hurt me, and that I need not worry!

A year after my grandmother's spiritual visit, I met a middle aged woman who worked as a supervisor for a school district in Virginia. We became friends through work, and one day she explained her psychic abilities to me. She was psychic and could read many things about a person, in a way similar to my grandmother. Initially, she suggested that I develop my own skills, and she expressed an interest in training me. Still, I was afraid to grow and develop them as she recommended, so I stopped. However, she always enjoyed hearing my comments about fellow diners as we talked during meals in dining rooms. She thought my grandmother had done excellent work guiding me.

Over the next thirty years, my life was a busy one. It consisted of raising a family, having a divorce, marrying my second wife, owning and operating several businesses. During this time I used my intuitive abilities to assist me as I made a variety of decisions.

In 1985, I started to write a book entitled "Angel". It was about a woman gifted with the ability to heal others through the touch of her hand. News of her ability quickly spread, making her life a public spectacle and gradually impossible to live normally. Even the military became interested in her skills, and kidnapped her for their use on upper level officers. During the writing of this novel, I became stuck when the woman was attempting an escape. Unfortunately, I never finished writing this book. This was one of my earliest forays into writing in the metaphysical genre.

In 1999, I finally began to seriously study metaphysics after I received a reading from Bob Bens. As a result of his reading, I took several of his classes. Bob is a gifted medium who gave me the impetus to learn all that I could of the metaphysical world. During a Development Circle class that Bob Bens taught, I met Beverly Stone, another very talented and gifted reader.

In early 2005, Beverly sent Brother Harold to me. She had her own guide who was a monk. I asked her if she could find out from her guide if he had any friends who were monks who might be interested in becoming one of my guides. The following week, she indicated to me that Brother Harold was interested.

At that time, no one knew that he was also a healer and everyone thought he was just a studious monk. I first noticed the effect his presence had as one of my Spirit Guides when my blood pressure dropped to normal levels even though it had been elevated for over 20 years. I began to notice a calmness which would occasionally overcome me, and I am thankful to Brother Harold for this change as well.

My discovery of Brother Harold's healing abilities is outlined in the following chapters. I ask you to consider how it emotionally impacted on me when I watched him cutting up a heart and I sat there fully believing this patient was about to die! I tell you this now, to let you know what is imminent within these pages, so you can be prepared.

My deceased mother, a registered nurse, was available to me in spirit form. Her spirit communicated to me what was taking place and let me know that everything would be okay. Her calming presence reassured me as I sat there watching Brother Harold's heart dissection instead of running wildly from the house as my instinct would have had me do!

I wish to define spirit. Some people are confused by its meaning, not knowing if it refers to dead people, corpses, or some other supernatural creature. For now, please relax and open your mind to some unique ideas. Generally, most people agree that every single human being on earth was created by God. This is so, and we all have lives to lead on earth, with a reason for living.

All human beings on earth are also spirits. You may want to define it as spirit energy, life force, a piece of God, or use whatever description works. When this life on earth has ended and our body passes on, the spirit within us lives forever. It becomes energy, and this spiritual energy can accomplish many things. Each spirit does not have a brain in the normal physical sense, but does have a personality and the memories it may choose to take with it from its life on earth. These memories and facts can be transferred before passing if a person wishes to do that. Unexpected deaths may eliminate that possibility, which could cause a memory problem that may take years to straighten out.

Since I was born and raised in New York City, being able to observe just about anything one can see of life in a big city, has probably been one of the biggest advantages for my spiritual development. I rarely flinch at some of the most unusual scenes and situations that I have been privileged to witness. Please prepare yourself to do the same unerring acceptance of what is truly unique as you travel with me through my journey in this book!

I thank God daily since I have been able to be a part of Brother Harold's life during this past year. I hope our journey continues for a very long time to come!

CHAPTER 1 - A NEW HEART

A human heart appeared before me.

I watched, fascinated, as Brother Harold, with no explanation, sliced the heart in half and opened it. Abruptly, my delight in being involved with Brother Harold's healing turned to abject terror and revulsion. I was thoroughly convinced that the patient was being killed!

Uneasily, I thought about leaving when my mother's energy suddenly materialized. Her appearance brought me an immense amount of comfort and reassurance. Before she crossed over in 1989, she was a registered nurse. Her favorite learning activity while training in nursing school had been to assist surgeons during operations. Sadly, after she completed her nursing training, she found little time to continue surgical assisting. Seeing her now, while watching Brother Harold in the middle of an operation, brought back loving memories of her.

Through clairvoyant communication, she let me know that Brother Harold was working on a duplicate of the 92 year old patient's heart. She assured me universal laws were at work that I was unaware of. Mother suggested that I should trust and continue to work with Brother Harold.

In a brief moment, she had put me at ease. No one else could have done it as quickly and effortlessly. Because my faith in her honesty and her nursing ability is unshakable, I was able to relax. I continued to watch the most incredible psychic surgery.

1

My mother reminded me how I had enjoyed working on ship models in my youth, and the kits I used to put them together. She compared my ship building hobby to Brother Harold's spirit work on duplicates of human organs. Obviously, Brother Harold's spirit could duplicate any organ exactly, perform whatever "operation" was needed on the duplicate, and, as I was later to learn, replace the original with its newly improved version in a blink of an eye.

I wondered where this knowledge came from. Truly, this was more than a simple "yes" to the question of "Is there life on other planets?" What a memorable day this had turned out to be!

Total time elapsed? Sixteen minutes.

This 92 year old woman had just received a replacement valve in her heart. Her heart's overall size had been reduced to improve the efficiency of blood flow through it, sewn together and finally inserted in place of the old, poorly functioning heart. Brother Harold watched her heart operate for a few minutes to make sure it functioned properly as nature had originally meant it to.

In a few moments, I "returned" to my waking life and realized that less than twenty-five minutes had passed. I was completely dumbfounded! There were so many things that I needed to think about and I decided that hot, strong coffee this morning was definitely a requirement!

The operation had been performed in a woman's home while she was fast asleep. Not one drop of blood was lost, her chest had not been surgically opened, and she was unaware that an operation had been performed at the psychic/energetic level. No operating room, no anesthesiologist, no hospital. Life was truly amazing!

The only words that Brother Harold uttered was at the end of her "surgery", just before he was about to leave. His commentary? "She has been receiving terrible medical treatment in Louisiana!"

CHAPTER 2 – FIRST MESSAGE

A story such as this begs for a beginning! Let me return to 1999 and tell you how I embarked on this unusual tale.

Six years ago, in 1999, I had my first encounter with the spirit world through a local and talented medium. When I asked to gain some insight on the spirit world, he gave me a reading. I found this reading to be very thought provoking, and I asked him what classes were available to educate myself about mediums. In response, this gentleman let me know that he was starting a new class within the month. I signed up!

I continued to attend these classes for over a year. He introduced us to the principles of Natural Law, the spirit world, as well as all of it idiosyncrasies. Logically, I found that these laws made perfect sense. I welcomed the concept of living forever and making full use of lifelong learning. Having previously lost some opportunities to do so on earth, I became determined to not lose the same opportunities in the spirit world. Learning to communicate with spirits, using symbols, and other non-spoken terms was a more difficult challenge. This has continued to be a long learning curve I entered, and continue to enjoy.

Once the class was completed, some of us wanted to continue to meet in discussion groups and further expand our knowledge among ourselves. A group of ten students, including myself, began to meet weekly at my house in what we dubbed the Development Circle. Meeting regularly is a normal event within metaphysical circles.

We communicated with spirits weekly, exchanging the messages that we received with each other, and continued to learn through our experiences. Very quickly, it became obvious to us that we all were on different paths and learning at different speeds. We each had different abilities, unique to ourselves, which is one of the most fascinating properties about metaphysics. Our Development Circle continued to gather weekly until the spring of 2005.

Early one morning that spring, I was slowly waking up in bed, planning my day. Suddenly, new information from a spirit flooded into my mind. I realized that this was a spirit that I had not communicated with before! This awareness happened within a matter of seconds. This reception of instantaneous knowledge can happen very quickly, much like receiving a spirit fax! Only, this was a "spirit fax" which contained very elaborate information that I absorbed and understood within seconds.

Spirits are wonderful entities! It was amazing how much I learned at that moment in time. Suddenly, I knew that I could travel anywhere I wanted with this spirit. He let me know that there were no limits except those that were self-imposed. Later, I realized that there was a plan to this sudden influx of new information. I gradually understood that I had been chosen to be a channel for this spirit, and now I needed to be trained.

I was quite impressed, but I had no idea which spirit was communicating with me. I decided that I would run through my list of spirit guides, speaking each name out loud, hoping that something would happen when I hit the right one. As I went through my list of

6

known spirit guides, I finally came to Brother Harold's name. As soon as I said his name, Brother Harold's blue spirit energy instantly appeared in my vision. Immediately, I felt thankful because I knew that he was a very intelligent and noble spirit. I gladly welcomed him, and we began to have intense discussions.

Over the next five days, without fail, we communicated daily. Every day I asked numerous questions, and Brother Harold answered them immediately. I had the strong impression that he wanted to share with me information that I could communicate to the Development Circle participants each Wednesday.

I went one step further and asked Brother Harold if I could channel his knowledge so that they could be put into a book that could be shared with many people. My eyes were closed as I asked this question. As I quietly made my request, I could sense his blue energy on my left side. Immediately, three individual bright bolts of golden light emerged from his energy and shot to the upper right side of my vision!

A brilliant sun formed and began spreading its warm light out from the upper right side. I had never had a question answered so powerfully, so quickly, or so forcefully before. It was then that I realized I was in the presence of a brilliant spirit, one who communicated very effectively to me.

With a great deal of excitement, on the following Wednesday I addressed the Development Circle, and explained the concept of channeling Brother Harold. I received a lot of positive feedback and support from everyone. I then related the following message from Brother Harold to the group:

Brother Harold has asked me to explain his thoughts to you; they are meant to be of assistance to all of us, and meant in a very positive manner.

First, he rejoices in the fact that we are all spirits; each one of us hearing this and Brother Harold himself. We were each created by the One original force of all good and we were all created to exist as spirits forever.

He suggests that we all celebrate that fact.

He adds to that the fact that those of us at this meeting on earth currently share a life as humans; this adds one new event to celebrate and rejoice in. Brother Harold points out that there are many different ways of viewing the situation; he chooses the above view and asks us to join him in celebrating the goodness, simplicity and truth of it.

CHAPTER 3 – SECOND MESSAGE

After relating my message from Brother Harold to the Development Circle, I took a deep breath and relaxed. While taking a few minutes during the meeting to relax, my mind wandered off and I lost track of what was happening in the Development Circle. A little while later, I refocused my attention to the meeting.

Lions! I was absolutely stunned to suddenly see a room filled with them. They were all lying down, quietly facing in my direction. There were rows and rows of them! From floor to ceiling there were lions. Male Lions, female lions, cubs, and mixed in I saw a raccoon and some other animals.

Staring at the animals, I realized after some very long minutes that I was seeing them as a vision. I had no idea what was happening, or why I was even seeing them! At this point, I began to concentrate and went into another trance. The animals vanished.

At the next meeting, on the following Wednesday evening, I saw the lions again. Right after the opening of the meeting, the lions reappeared. This time, all the lions and other animals sat directly in front of me. The large male lion at the center was close enough to lean forward and sniff me. I found this to be very unnerving and exciting at the same time! This time, I was not afraid.

Instead, I was very excited to have a lion in spirit form in front of me! What I found extremely interesting was how I observed none of the problems which would ordinarily be caused by several very heavy animals lying on top of each other. Now I realized, after seeing this

9

unusual vision, in the metaphysical and spiritual realm anything was possible!

Again, I was distracted by other things occurring during the meeting. It was not until the next morning when, during my daily communication with Brother Harold, that I asked him to explain the significance of seeing a roomful of lions. Brother Harold responded with the following message for me to share with the Circle:

Notice the lions and raccoons.

They are mounded on top of each other, yet they are comfortable. This could not happen on earth, but in spirit, anything is possible.

This visual tapestry creates a picture that earthlings can easily remember. God created all animals as he created all humans, to operate together, not apart.

My life on earth and what I have seen on earth from the spirit world has convinced me that people need to be reminded of the spirit of togetherness and cooperation. God has a purpose for making man in this way.

Look around yourself and remember the picture of the lions.

10

CHAPTER 4 – THE PRACTICE OF SPIRIT MEDICINE

How does one practice spirit healing? This is a very common question!

Brother Harold and I have a regular routine that we have established over many months. Normally, I awaken early, and prepare myself to begin at 5:00 am. I begin by stating an Affirmation. When dealing with the spirit world, it is good to state your intent upon arrival to set the stage for future acts so they can be interpreted correctly. By speaking my Affirmation first, this is my way to let the spirit world know that my intent is pure. I am a Godly person seeking to help others, meaning no harm to anyone. I am asking to be judged based on this Affirmation.

Every Development Circle meeting held on Wednesday nights is opened with a prayer, which followed by us all stating our intent for the meeting. This is a good way to work with spirits.

I begin with the same Affirmation each time:

I am surrounded by love.

My forces are here.
I will have my heart's desire as soon as God sees fit.

I close myself to all that it negative and undeveloped,
I open myself to all that is pure and holy.

The Lord is in my holy temple,

Let there be peace, peace, peace.

I am spirit, I am free,

Nothing but good can come to me.

Once my intent is stated, I summon my faithful spirit guides. Dr. Price, the first guide I summon, is my chemist spirit guide. His purpose is to monitor and regulate my physical energy level, to ensure enough reserves are available for Brother Harold to use for his work, and enough for me to use in my daily life. My sole purpose for channeling Brother Harold is to allow him to use my energy. Spirits consist of energy. They have enough for their own use, but not enough to expend easily while doing sophisticated healing tasks as Brother Harold does.

The physical human body is designed to create its own energy through eating and digesting foods and exercising. Channeling with Brother Harold uses energy from my physical body, which places demands on it above what is normally taken from it in daily life. When Brother Harold is about to use too much of my energy, Dr. Price lets us all know that we should stop. Dr. Price monitors these levels carefully, for drawing too much energy from me would be exhausting and could make me ill. Dr. Price does an excellent job balancing this flow of energy, and when it becomes too low, he will notify all of us so that we will stop!

Afterwards, I usually sleep for a few hours to regenerate my strength. Early on in my channeling experiences with Brother Harold, we had a few times where it was difficult to monitor the correct level of energy being used in my body. A few times we used too much and I felt very drained and exhausted afterwards as a result. Fortunately, that was corrected easily by getting extra rest and I had no lingering damage.

Next, I summon Two Feathers, my Native American guide, who is a warrior spirit that has taken the role of protecting me. Two Feathers, my Native American spirit guide, is present to provide protection for us. One patient that we were assisting, who was diagnosed with Fibromyalgia, is a prime example of how Two Feathers sheltered us. Suddenly, with no warning, an element of her disease started viciously attacking me! Two Feathers rapidly jumped into action by placing shields in front of me. He then quickly struck back, and after a short battle, he finally killed the attacking entity. He does a great job of silently providing protection, and is never intrusive while Brother Harold is working.

Finally, I summon Brother Harold who is a monk. Quite some time ago, he was a monk on earth in the Catholic Church. From other spirits, also fellow monks, he had the reputation of being very studious. That information was given to me as he became my spirit guide.

How did I meet Brother Harold? A friend, who is a fellow member of the Wednesday group, had a monk guide. One day I asked her to find out from her guide if he had a brother monk who would like to be my guide. I felt drawn to monks, and I believed that a spirit monk guide would be a good addition to the spirits that I communicated with. Her monk guide answered by telling her that Brother Harold had expressed an interest in working with me. He added that Brother Harold is a very studious monk!

I assume that when Brother Harold crossed over into the spirit world that was when he started to study medicine. He has become a very knowledgeable surgeon, as you will soon see! I learned that the spirit world offers schools allowing studies in many disciplines. Medicine is so different in the spirit world, it would require a great deal to time to study it.

Let me say that I have interested Brother Harold. I have felt fortunate from the very first day to have been chosen to work with him. Rather than asking a variety of questions, I have worked with him, learning new things each and every day and sending my thanks to God for this opportunity. The only reason I am with Brother Harold, is to enable him to draw on my energy, and to provide a physical support for Brother Harold to "lean on" while he performs his healing ministry.

Normally, all the spirit guides arrive immediately once I've requested their presence. After everyone has arrived, I then provide the name of the person we plan to visit, and I speak about their medical conditions or concerns. This may take a few quick seconds, or minutes, to explain. When we are ready, I repeat the person's name, and we then set off.

Once we have begun traveling, I see nothing until we are in the presence of our patient. I will only see the outer body if Brother Harold plans to work on the exterior portion of the body, such as an injured arm or leg. Generally, the external sections of the body only require healing energy sent to them from Brother Harold.

If the medical concern is within the body, such as the heart, blood vessels, lungs, eyes and other areas, a visit into the internal portion of the body is required. Brother Harold and I have occasionally examined the chest or heart area, arteries, sometimes even the grey matter in the brain.

Brother Harold is a spirit and takes up very little space. The part of me that travels with him is also very small. This tiny part of me has the ability to communicate, has vision, contains energy and is somewhat mobile. I have followed Brother Harold into blood veins and brains of our patients. The "human" portion of Roger, who sits in North Carolina with a blinder over his eyes, can see the spiritual part of himself traveling, observing and occasionally working with Brother Harold.

I would like to explain the differences between medical practice on Earth, which most people understand, and medical practice at the spiritual level which very few people are familiar with. On Earth, everyone understands the concept of visiting their doctor when they become ill, break a bone or have a regular examination for personal care. Medical practice at the spiritual level involves doctors who will also look over your body but at a spiritual level.

Everyone is familiar with the television program *Star Trek* and the notion of beaming people from one location to another. The idea of quickly disappearing from one location, taking apart all the cells of a body in the process, then rematerializing somewhere else with all the human body cells put back together again in exactly the same order, is intriguing! To our minds, it is an amazing and almost impossible to believe task.

In a very similar way spirit healers are able to obtain, very quickly, an identical copy of anything they need. Creating a copy of a heart, or a complete copy of a skeleton, is no problem within spirit medicine. Once "created", this identical copy can be worked on, repaired, or redesigned to work more efficiently. After the repairs have been made, the copy is used to replace the original organ or body part. This replacement happens instantaneously, without the use of anesthesia, without making an incision in the body, and without losing one drop of blood.

Think of the time and energy saved. patient safety, and the potential for healing the elderly or infirm without putting them through the strain of surgery at the physical level!

In some cases, Brother Harold has acquired a replacement heart, spine, or a certain nerve for replacement. In one case, he noticed that the bones of a patient were badly in need of calcium which would strengthen the bones and help prevent them from breaking. Brother Harold obtained a replacement skeleton of the woman, sprayed it down with calcium several times, and then proceeded to substitute the woman's skeleton with its strengthened replacement.

Many times I have wondered where these medical advances came from. These techniques were not developed here on earth. A long-distance travel with Brother Harold to watch him perform brain surgery on an alien provided me with hints of the origination of some of these unusual techniques. Perhaps a hundred years from now, these new procedures will be commonplace here on earth. For today, they are commonplace in Brother Harold's world.

CHAPTER 5 – ALZHEIMER'S

My telephone rang early one morning. To my surprise, an old friend that I did not expect to call me was speaking anxiously.

"Roger, can you and Brother Harold help me? My grandfather has recently been diagnosed with Alzheimer's, and I don't know what to do," she implored through tears.

"That can be a tough one, but let me see where we are. I will get back to you," I gently responded.

I had worked with Alzheimer's a few times previously with Brother Harold, and I knew we could help if it was early enough during the progression of the disease. Sadly, I knew that when the mind has lost vital information, it is irrevocably gone.

The next morning at 5:00 am, Brother Harold and I went to see Andrew, my friend's grandfather. I informed Brother Harold that he had recently been diagnosed with Alzheimer's, and his family had requested an evaluation of what we could do to help him. Without a word from Brother Harold, we proceeded.

As Brother Harold began to look over Andrew's body, I attempted to tune into his thoughts. Physically he was asleep, yet Andrew was worried about precious memories he might forget, and he kept repeating to himself various family names and facts about each family member that he wanted so urgently to remember.

It was a touching moment for me to witness the beginnings of his struggle against a frightening disease he had just learned about and was inexperienced with, one which would ultimately win. I began to feel that we were badly needed to bring this man some ease within his troubled mind.

Brother Harold began to work on Andrew's brain. Prior experience has shown me that Brother Harold excels in this area. He immediately started to eliminate parts, changing sections, and medicating various areas. Watching an experienced organist playing a multi-tiered organ with foot pedals is a good analogy to use as I watched Brother Harold begin to "play" this gentleman's Alzheimer-infused brain. His work was done as quickly and precisely as an organist strikes a series of melodic keys while moving his feet in time to different pedals. I am always astonished by both an experienced organist's skills as well as Brother Harold's abilities! His ability to understand the human brain and to work on it quickly, without the aid of a microscope or machine, with no anesthesiologist present, is always a wonder to behold.

Suddenly, Brother Harold collected all of the memories Andrew was valiantly working with, all the while adding additional memories from his brain. He created a vortex of information which was placed into a new section of Andrew's brain where it could be stored. In this part of the brain, Alzheimer's would be unable to destroy Andrew's memories, and he would be able to access this information at will. Ultimately, that was Brother Harold's plan for Andrew, which was "spirit faxed" to me.

"Spirit fax" is the term I use to describe "intuitive thought". When a spirit communicates with you, since he consists of energy, the spirit does not have a mouth, tongue, voice box, or lungs, which would normally be used to "speak". His method of communicating with me is by transferring thoughts into my mind. It is possible to form words, but that requires experience and a lot of energy on the spirit's part. Transferring thoughts is a lot easier and more natural for the spirit to use as a method of effective communication. The ability to receive thoughts and to understand what they are is a new experience for humans. Someone without any experience or comprehension of spirit communication will often think they are imagining the thoughts or pictures that suddenly appear in their mind. A person with experience in this unique method of communicating with another will start to enjoy the process and revel in its ease.

After we completed this session with Andrew, I quietly sat and mulled over my thoughts as I drank coffee and reviewed the thirty minutes that I had just spent with Brother Harold. Was I the luckiest person alive to be able to experience these things and witness them? I began to assess exactly what he had done and what I could recollect from what I had garnered from his thoughts. This evaluation report to Andrew's family would be longer than Brother Harold's treatment!

This was only the third Alzheimer's patient we had worked on, so there is no final word on the results of our visit yet. Intuitively, what I do know is that Andrew will do alright, now that Brother Harold has done the work necessary to help preserve his memories.

Whether his lifespan will be as long as someone without Alzheimer's, I do not know.

CHAPTER 6 – THE BRAIN TUMOR

One quiet Thursday morning while I was relaxing, the telephone buzzed. It was Laura, a friend I knew from the Wednesday evening Development Circle meetings.

She was terribly upset and concerned about her mother, Agatha. I spoke with her and learned some bad news. Apparently, when Brother Harold and I had visited Laura's energy earlier, the brain tumor I had seen there was occurring in her mother and not Laura. She then asked if Brother Harold and I could visit her mom to do whatever we could to help.

The next morning, after I connected to Brother Harold and told him about Agatha's health concern, he and I went to visit her energy. She lived in Idaho, but distance is no problem for us and within two seconds we were there viewing her energy. While we were observing her energy form, Brother Harold flattened it so that it appeared to us as a two dimensional surface. We started to examine it closely, moving in a counter-clockwise manner. As we carefully looked at her flattened energy form, we occasionally encountered some small, black, seed-like objects. Intuitively, I understood that they were cancer cells which had metastasized throughout her body. At this point, I became very afraid for Agatha!

Brother Harold stopped our forward movement and a viewing screen was installed in front of us. We restarted our motion and began to move in a clockwise direction. Brother Harold busily sprayed clear liquid onto Agatha's form as we advanced. As we slowly moved forward, I could see the seed-like objects. Continuing on, the clear liquid spray showered the entire area. At this point, the objects then passed underneath the viewing screen. As I looked at Agatha through the viewing screen, I saw the affected areas and noticed that they no longer had the black seek-like objects embedded within. To my amazement, they had completely vanished! Brother Harold's spray had simply destroyed and removed them.

After we completed spraying the entire area affected by these seed-like objects, I asked to see her whole energy form. We backed up, and I could see the entire area, which proved to be completely seed-free. Intuitively, I knew her energy form was now good, clean, and healthy as it should be.

Then, I saw the organs from her body, which was encased in a circle. Brother Harold was spraying them with a darker liquid that became foam-like and lingered for a few minutes. Once Brother Harold had completed spraying Agatha's internal organs, I returned to full awareness in my home as I opened my eyes.

I sat in my chair and reflected on this morning's incidents for a long time, wondering exactly what had happened.

However, I realized that I DID know what had transpired. I was amazed, and filled with awe. Brother Harold had completely astonished me and helped me realize how simple things were. Reflecting, I had known for years that the simple solution almost always works.

Life is simple; disease cures can be just as simple.

Curing the cancer that is spreading all over Agatha's body can be as simple as spraying the right medicine on the cancer, ending the problem once and for all.

CHAPTER 7 – SAVING HILLARY

Early one Friday morning at eight o'clock, Hillary called. I had known her for a month in the Development Circle meetings she had attended, but was surprised to hear from her at this hour.

She was somewhat breathless as she described her problem. She had been up all night, kept awake by her heart which had been pounding very fast. She had eaten some nuts the previous night and attributed her fast heartbeat to a reaction from eating nuts and to her continuing illness, Fibromyalgia. She was a registered nurse who had left her vocation in protest to the manner in which a majority of doctors treated their patients. As she finished speaking, her final pleading question "Could Brother Harold help me?" moved me.

In three minutes Brother Harold and I were there. Hillary was very agitated, as anyone who had been up all night would be. She was very worried about all the problems she could possibly be having. Brother Harold began his session by the use of his rays of soothing energy that were meant to calm her down and were showered over her body. After five minutes, the rays slowed down and vanished. I knew she was calm at last. The next twenty minutes were devoted to treatment of her Fibromyalgia.

Afterwards, I called Hillary to see how she felt. She acknowledged that she felt a lot better, but was still having faster than normal heart beats. This time, she mentioned a disc in her spine that might be out of position which could be causing pain in a rib behind her left breast. We went back.

Her rib was fine, but there was a disc out of alignment. It was quickly set back in line and Brother Harold followed up with energy treatments of the affected areas. A return call to Hillary indicated that she had more relief, but she requested a visit later that afternoon to see if we could address her faster than normal heart beat. I agreed to return with Brother Harold.

At 2:30 p.m., we were back. I was interested to see how Brother Harold would address her concerns about her fast heartbeat. Discussions prior to treatment have not been a part of our program!

Again, I was caught off guard as a purple colored glass-like object was slid into place over her heart. As Brother Harold looked through it, I was trying to do the same. I could see that this "plate" enlarged the view of the heart, but it did more than that. It showed the outside of the heart and what was happening just below the surface. Intuitively, I received a message and understood that he was examining the initiation of the electrical charge that kept the heart beating at a regular pace. I knew from past experiences that this electrical charge would be initiated somewhere in the heart, in a different place for each person.

The purple plate was removed and the heart received treatment in a tiny area at the bottom and in one small section at the top of her heart. Brother Harold used a medication which colored each of these sections green. We watched the heart continue to beat for a few minutes more, to make sure no further problems arose.

Our work was done. I had already scheduled an appointment with Hillary for 5:00 a.m. Monday morning to continue with additional

28

treatments. Making three visits in one day to a single patient was a first time experience for me, but in this case I felt it was sorely needed.

Saturday and Sunday went by with no calls from Hillary, so I assumed that we had done well and she should be resting comfortably.

Monday morning arrived, and we returned to Hillary. This time, Brother Harold took me into a dark place within her body. I was trying to figure out where we were when I suddenly saw a very small light ahead of us as Brother Harold went quickly through the vein we were in. Quickly, I threw off my inclination to become claustrophobic, knowing that to become anxious and agitated myself would do our patient no good. We continued through the tunnel, and I realized what we would soon come up to. Apparently, I had not realized that the purple glass showed arteries around the heart as well.

The tunnel widened and suddenly we saw small rocks ahead. Initially, I saw them scattered about the bottom of the tunnel. Gradually, the number of rocks increased, and I saw more rocks appearing on top of rocks. Soon, they were all throughout the tunnel and the passageway opening was almost invisible. At this point, we were moving very slowly. As we trudged along, I realized that Brother Harold was removing the rocks in some way but he was not shooting at them from the hip. I cannot visually see Brother Harold as he works. I only see what existed before our work and the results afterwards. While Brother Harold was somehow removing these rocks, it occurred to me that if he were to set all of this material free in the blood stream, it could cause a heart attack.

We continued on and on, through intersections where the clogging of the veins appeared to make them almost impassable. I realized that we were working to prevent a very massive heart attack that was about to occur!

After we had been working on Hillary's veins in her heart for over an hour, my chemist informed me that we should end this session before I started to experience energy problems. I told Brother Harold we needed to end, and I rejoined the physical world.

I phoned Hillary to tell her what we had done and promised to revisit her the next day to ensure that she had the cleanest vessels in the city! Her laughter made me feel good.

I took a three hour nap to refresh myself. Brother Harold had been working hard and had needed to use a lot of my energy reserves. When I woke up, I instinctively knew that we had done a good job; we had helped prevent what could have been a fatal heart attack! There had been so much blockage in her arteries, it was almost certain that death would have occurred.

Brother Harold's work on her heart to adjust the electrical impulses that regulated its beat could add years to an already productive life. There are plans in everyone's life which can affect the outcome not only of a person's life, but also the accomplishments during their life. I am gratified that I can assist so many people reach their goals.

CHAPTER 8 – DRIVING TO FLORIDA

Dan and Mary were in their mid-sixties when they began their annual drive in November from their house in Minnesota to their condo in sunny Florida. They left to travel south after the hurricane season was over and would happily return to their summer home in Minnesota in the spring. They made the biannual trek willingly, for never again did they want to go through the fear of weathering another hurricane! Mary thought about her blessings daily and was grateful to her husband who had agreed to live in Minnesota at her father's old house until almost Christmas every year. December was a wonderful time of year to spend in Florida.

They had been on the road driving for two long days and were about to stop for a much needed break to eat lunch. Before their departure, they had jotted down their favorite restaurants and planned their usual stops on each trip. Dan, with a forty year engineer's history, was a perfectionist, and preferred to have his route well planned out. Since this was a familiar trip for both of them, they regularly made the same stops, visited the same familiar hotels, traveled the same roads, and followed the same schedule.

Each time Dan and Mary traveled, he drove since Mary had not driven a car in fifteen years. She found that she was too nervous to drive, and they were both considerably more relaxed when she was able to be the passenger enjoying the views!

One day at noon, as they neared the end of their journey south, Dan pulled into the parking lot of a familiar restaurant, comforted by the "sameness" feeling he had. This last leg of their long drive had been a tough one, and he knew that he would have to stretch his stiff muscles when he got out of the car. Mary began her pre-lunch search of her purse for necessary items, things they needed during lunch and the bathroom break after lunch. Dan turned off the car and quickly got out to stretch his muscles.

On his third whole body stretch, he moved his foot to turn around but suddenly Dan lost his balance and fell! He collapsed to the ground hitting it with an unnerving thump.

Pain followed quickly as he lay there on the concrete. Dan's shoulder hurt, but what was worse was the realization that he was feeling severe shooting pains in his hip! Dan is a small-boned person who is in very good physical shape. He religiously exercised three times weekly and went on extended walks twice a week, both in Florida and in Minnesota. The exercises and the walking schedule would have to be amended, was one of Dan's first thoughts.

Over the next hour, Dan's pain intensified. The restaurant's manager and his assistant were both large people who had no problem helping Dan up and assisting him into the restaurant. Within half an hour, he was in the emergency clinic being examined by the local doctor. It didn't take very long to discover that Dan had broken his hip and would need surgery. Dan decided that he wanted to wait until he could get to Florida and consult his physician there before undergoing surgery. His pressing need was to get pain medicine for temporary relief so they could be on their way heading south quickly.

Mary suddenly found herself in the driver's seat while Dan sat crookedly in the passenger seat. He sat, drinking McDonald's coffee while giving her the occasional directions and advice on driving. Mary struggled with this unexpected change to their routine and fervently hoped that she would be able to manage the rest of their trip south safely.

The pain medication finally silenced Dan, and he slept peacefully while she nervously drove onward. She planned the next stop at the motel, registered, got the assistance of one large man to carry Dan to their room, moved their luggage into the room, and settled her husband as comfortably as she could. After she had planned it all through her mind twice, including giving Dan a wash down in bed and a light dinner and finally a pill to sleep on, she knew she could do it and her self confidence grew.

The rest of their trip to Florida was one that was fit for only the toughest Marine to handle. From Dan's point of view, only a strong dose of liquid morphine could kill the pain he felt in his hip. Coupled with a car in the hands of an inexperienced driver, the jerking as Mary moved between the gas and brake pedals caused a great deal of bouncing, which grated painfully over Dan's broken hip bones. Even a toughened Marine would have been challenged.

Mary finally ended the next day with Dan at his orthopedist's office. Dan had already telephoned ahead and they were awaiting his arrival. He was examined promptly and sent to the hospital in an ambulance to await surgery the next day.

The following Monday, I received a call from Miriam, who had spoken to Dan's daughter and was a good friend of hers. She related the story of Mary and Dan's incredible journey to me. Dan had just returned home to recuperate after his operation on Saturday. Miriam asked me if Brother Harold and I could help Dan's bones heal.

Promptly, Brother Harold and I arrived and examined Dan's hip. We were able to see all of his broken hip bones. Brother Harold concentrated on his left side, sending powerful healing energy in waves to his bones. The broken bones in question were colored yellow, probably as a result of the spirit medication that Brother Harold used. Historically, this coloration wears off as the bones heal, which normally occurs within three to four days.

What I found amazing was to see how small Dan's bones were. He appeared to be a small man, but had muscles that were in excellent tone. The injured muscles were located in a small area of his thigh below his hip. Brother Harold followed the healing energy sent to his bones with additional healing energy that was meant to relieve the pain in his muscles. This treatment lasted thirty minutes.

At 5:00 a.m. the next morning, we found Dan in the same position and began treating him again. The yellow color had faded on the bones, but was still visible. Twenty minutes into this treatment, Dan suddenly started moving and got out of bed. Puzzled, Brother Harold started looking around the room for him, but he was gone. We waited five minutes, but Dan never returned. He had simply gotten up and left!

34

I called my friend Miriam, and we laughed about the remarkable healing that had just occurred. There was no possible way that he was completely healed, but he was on his feet and had gone somewhere. She promised to call his daughter and get back to me.

The next day, Miriam called me back, in hysterics! She told me that Dan had gotten up, dressed himself and had gone out for breakfast. What was even more surprising? During that same afternoon, he and Mary had gone to a party at a friend's house which lasted late into the evening. He had even been dancing at the party with his wife!

This has to be the most remarkable healing that Brother Harold and I have ever participated in. I have seen patients who have had broken bones heal in six days, and I thought THAT was a remarkable feat!

Truly, Dan holds the record.

CHAPTER 9 – PETER'S FALL

One Wednesday night, after our regular Development circle meeting, Nina asked to talk to me with a worried expression on her face.

"Peter, who is my daughter's neighbor, had a terrible accident this morning at his job! He was standing on a forklift moving some boxes, when he stumbled and fell 20 feet onto a concrete floor. His head hit hard on the concrete and blood was coming out of one of his ears by the time he was picked up by an ambulance. They immediately flew Peter in a helicopter to the hospital in Chapel Hill! He had emergency surgery and is in intensive care now," she explained.

"What is his prognosis?" I asked.

"They are hopeful. They predict that Peter could spend several months in the hospital, including rehabilitation. But, they don't feel that he will be the same. Could Brother Harold possibly help him?" she asked.

"We will go right away," I answered.

Nina left and I immediately sat down to call my guides and Brother Harold. Within seconds, we were in Chapel Hill, moments later we were at Peter's side. There were still a lot of people present in his room that were monitoring him, and Peter had several IV's in his arms which were receiving multiple medications. His head was still open underneath the surgical dressing, so Brother Harold went to his brain, taking me along.

I was immediately lost, but Brother Harold was comfortably at home in his element. He began by looking over Peter's brain and quickly started treating him with energy bursts. At one point I watched Brother Harold as he closed wounds, at other times, I saw him cut and re-grow injured cells. The energy that he transmitted to Peter changed several times. It was obvious that he was using different energy to accomplish different tasks.

Spirit medical work is done quickly. In fifteen minutes, Brother Harold did what would have taken hours if earth-based doctors had the required knowledge to do the same work. Since Peter had already been through an operation, this must be new healing work Brother Harold was doing.

Then, we went outside his brain and started to work on Peter's shoulder and arm. Apparently, they had also been injured as he fell to the concrete floor.

While Brother Harold continued to apply healing energy, I began to receive Peter's thoughts. He was still unconscious, but he was thinking. Peter's thoughts were all about his wife and two children. His thoughts were all about the love he felt for them and the concern he felt that they would be so troubled for him. I was deeply touched. This was a nice man and we must help him for his family's sake and his own.

Soon after that, we left. I was still very touched by Peter's emotions. I called Nina to tell her what we had done and what impressions I had received from Peter. She confirmed everything I had "heard".

At 5:00 the next morning, we returned to Peter to do more healing work on his injuries. Peter was asleep in his room, alone, with no nurses or doctors around him. Again, we went into his brain. This time, the visit was mostly a look-see and follow up visit with very little action taken. Obviously, Brother Harold was pleased with his work. He devoted another ten minutes to his shoulder and arm, and then we departed.

The following Saturday, Sunday and Monday at 5:00 a.m. we returned to check on his progress. He had awakened Friday afternoon and was able to sit up in bed. Each day, each of our visits was shorter. No more work needed to be done on Peter's brain, less and less work was done on his shoulder and arm.

Tuesday afternoon, my phone rang. It was a breathless Nina!

"The hospital sent Peter home! His doctor said he had never seen anything like it before, but he was recovering nicely and could go home," she almost yelled with joy.

"Great news!" I exclaimed.

Once again, I was grateful that such a nice guy would be so fortunate. I thought of his children and wife and of how relieved they must be. It was a good day for me, definitely one worth celebrating! I thought of Brother Harold and the amazing work he had done on Peter's brain. No one would ever know what might have happened without Brother Harold there to help him.

CHAPTER 10 – "TERMINAL"

In November, I received a call from my friend Kate. She is a registered nurse and is married to a doctor. They had a friend, Bob, who was suffering from liver cancer and was labeled terminally ill with a prognosis of two to four weeks left to live. Fortunately, he was not in pain. He was prescribed a chemotherapy pill which was meant to attack the cancer in his liver, and Bob would probably need to take this pill daily until he died.

I let Kate know that Brother Harold and I would do our best to help Bob. The next morning at our usual 5:00 time, we started to work on him. I fully expected to see black seeds of cancer throughout his body. To my surprise, there were none! We did see a small amount of cancer on his liver which had withered away into two small pieces. These cancer cells showed up as yellow dots on the liver when Brother Harold examined it. He sprayed Bob's liver with medication that killed the remaining cancer cells immediately.

Afterwards, he treated Bob's withered and tiny liver with healing energy, carefully nursing it until it started to grow in size. When Brother Harold finished, the liver was twice the size than it had been. I felt good about what had been done and I reported our success to Kate who had referred us.

On the second morning, we went to see Bob, and when we got to his liver, it was reduced in size to the same two pieces that had been there the day before! I was furious! I assumed that he must be drinking alcohol, which was the only thing I could think of that could kill off his liver that quickly. I was upset because Brother Harold had nursed Bob's liver so carefully yesterday only to have our work been for naught.

I called Kate and asked her why he was still drinking. She was very quick to assure me that he was not drinking! Thinking for a moment, she wondered if it was caused by the chemotherapy pill he was taking daily. The pill would kill the cancer, but it must have been affecting his liver as well.

"Please understand – Brother Harold has killed the last cancer. He is now trying to regenerate the liver, but the chemotherapy drug is killing it. There is no cancer left to kill! Can you explain that to the doctors?" I asked, trying to mask my frustration.

"They may not believe that the cancer is dead" was her only response.

"You have given him two to four weeks to live. I am not asking for them to take a big chance!" I retorted.

Against my recommendations, the chemotherapy drug was continued. Brother Harold and I went to see Bob every three days to provide treatment. Each time we visited, we valiantly coddled these tiny pieces of liver in an effort to help Bob and to keep his liver alive.

When I asked additional questions, I discovered Bob also suffered from congestive heart failure, as well as retaining fluid in his abdomen which is a common side effect from liver disease. His doctor was draining off large amounts of fluid daily. Brother Harold started to treat him for heart failure and fluid retention. He asked me to keep him updated on the status of Bob's fluid drainage levels. After two additional treatments, Kate called me to report that Bob's daily fluid drainage levels were decreasing! Kate was thrilled, and the doctor couldn't explain why this was happening.

Bob lived for three additional months, which was far longer than Bob's original two to four week life expectancy. Between Christmas and New Year's that year, he felt well enough to go with his grown sons on a trip to South America. After he returned, Bob's hospice care providers began to support him with end-of-life care. There are certain predicators they will use to estimate the prognosis for their patients.

During the first week of February, hospice informed Bob's family that he might pass away the next day, which was a Saturday. All the obvious signs pointed to this end. A week later, his family was questioning how and why he was still alive! The amount of fluid retained in his abdomen was down to almost nothing on a daily basis. At one point during his disease, there had been almost five quarts drawn off daily! The doctor and nurse were utterly confused! Brother Harold and I continued to treat Bob.

March 2006 arrived, and with no obvious explanation, Bob was still alive enjoying basketball games on television. To everyone's surprise, he got out of bed one day and announced to everyone that he felt better! This lasted for about two weeks until he passed away on March 11, 2006.

Frequently, I am reminded that he had originally been given two to four weeks to live. With Brother Harold's help, he enjoyed about four more months of life, which fortunately was pain free. He was able to spend his last days enjoying a meaningful life with his family and friends.

When I reflect back on those days, I often wonder what real difference we might have made in Bob's life if his chemotherapy drug protocol had been stopped.

CHAPTER 11 – THE ALIEN'S BRAIN

When I am ready to start working on a patient and summon Brother Harold, I usually wait until I see his sky blue color appear in my sight. At that point, I know he is here with me.

On this particular morning, at approximately 11 o'clock, I was sitting at my desk getting ready to pay bills. I closed my eyes for a minute as I was clearing my mind, and I saw lots of sky blue in my vision. After a few minutes, it was still sitting there. Intuitively, I felt that Brother Harold was there and he wanted me to go somewhere with him.

At this point I realized my bill-paying plans were about to change! I summoned my chemist and my Native American, and I told Brother Harold we were ready to go. My blinders were in place, and I saw nothing. Before I started, I had noticed the time – it was 11:13 a.m.

Suddenly, a long strip of paper, about three inches wide appeared a foot below my vision. I choose my words carefully, because I am still not entirely sure exactly what part of me travels with Brother Harold. I do know that I am able to see certain things, perhaps the real reason for explaining the "third eye" concept.

This unusually shaped paper contained writing which was not in any language I was familiar with. It held a language that was apparently dependent on symbols and visual clues for meaning. Intuitively, I wondered whether this was a spirit language that was easily learned by people from many different places.

The paper was quite long, and contained quite a bit of writing. For some reason, I assumed it was a list of directions to the place we were going. It must be very complicated to require this many directions! Normally, it takes us two seconds to get to Miami, seven seconds to get to California, and eleven seconds to get to Iraq. There were some of the trips I had taken with Brother Harold. Today's trip proved to be quite different!

When we finally stopped moving, I lifted my eye cover quickly to check my clock. It was 11:28. We had been traveling for fifteen minutes! I was exhilarated, but not without a bit of fear. I was physically sitting at my desk in North Carolina. Part of my consciousness was with Brother Harold, my chemist and my Native American. Where the hell were we?

At this point I started to breathe deeply to calm myself down. Trusting Brother Harold is a given even if I was disturbed and completely lost. Gradually, things started to clear. Somehow, I realized that we were on another planet! Brother Harold "spirit faxed" reassurances to me, to let me know that I should relax and to keep up! There was no need to repeat the last part, as I was determined not to get lost.

Suddenly we went into a brain, and started to move forward inside it. I was following a small light and was staying very close to Brother Harold as we worked through this strange brain matter. I realized that we were moving fairly quickly considering where we were. As we kept moving, it occurred to me that this was one huge brain we were in! We traveled for approximately five minutes before I finally saw

46

some material that was colored yellow. I thought that this must be the result of medication that travels to a site, causing a color change. Perhaps this was a cancer site?

We stopped and Brother Harold started to cut. Within the next five minutes, the yellow matter had been excised and was efficiently removed. Brother Harold followed this "surgery" by giving this strange brain a short energy treatment before our visit ended. To my relief, our journey out and home was much faster!

Removing my blinders, I sat and thought about this unusual journey. With growing amazement, I realized that we had visited an alien's brain! I have been to many places while traveling with Brother Harold, but I never expected that I would take an interplanetary trip with him. Musing, I decided that Brother Harold must certainly enjoy an inter-planetary reputation for his excellent work on brains!

CHAPTER 12 – PAULA'S SKELETON

One day, I received a phone call from Paula. She had been referred to me by a mutual friend who was concerned for Paula. I discovered that Paula was a reasonably active and fairly healthy woman in her mid-sixties. However, she was complaining of quite a bit of pain in her knee. It had been injured in an accident and the pain was affecting her mobility and her ability to get around easily.

She and I talked and I explained how Brother Harold and I function together as a team to help people. Since Paula had experiences with spirits in her past, she was a full believer of spiritual medicine. When that is the case, it is always much simpler to describe to others how Brother Harold and I operate!

The next morning, Brother Harold gave her a complete examination. After he finished his assessment, we finished by giving her knee energy treatments for ten minutes. Afterwards, I felt satisfied, which has always been a good sign and tells me that the treatment has been effective.

The next two mornings, we repeated the treatment in the same manner. Later, I followed up with a call to Paula. She reported that she felt much better and was able to get to work and do her job with a lot less pain! I was very pleased, and suggested that Brother Harold and I visit her twice more before we were done. She agreed.

When we arrived the next morning, I was in for another surprise! After we began as we normally did, everything went black. A few seconds later, a skeleton suddenly appeared in my vision. Intuitively, I

49

sensed from Brother Harold that it was Paula's skeleton and it would be treated with some badly needed calcium.

He proceeded to spray her skeleton back and forth with some white powder, covering it from head to toe. Then Brother Harold repeated the process from foot to head. As the white powder hit her bones, in some areas it was instantly absorbed. Some parts of her bones did not absorb any of this white powdered calcium. The final result, after four sprayings, was a mottled skeleton.

It suddenly disappeared as it replaced the skeleton in her body. If one remembers the old Star Trek series where characters were frequently beamed from one location to another, Brother Harold must have access to a similar type of ability when he replaces organs or skeletons with their duplicates! The next morning I phoned Paula to let her know what had unexpectedly happened during her last treatment. She was quite pleased to know that her skeleton had been buffed up with calcium! Hopefully, with this treatment, future broken bones that could be incredibly debilitating for an elderly woman would be avoided.

CHAPTER 13 – DEBBIE AND HER ROBOT

One day a former patient called and asked me if Brother Harold could work on her sister, Debbie, in California. Debbie had been sick for several years and was currently living at home, disabled, confined to a wheelchair and unable to work. She suffered from Fibromyalgia, which I understand can lead to Lupus.

The next morning Brother Harold and I traveled to California so that we could work on Debbie. As Brother Harold was doing his initial examinations and treatments, I tuned into her thoughts. The first thing that I picked up was the thought of a high heeled shoe. This shoe kept appearing to me, over and over again. Then it appeared to me as a Cinderella slipper! She was dreaming of becoming like Cinderella, sharing the same dreams that Cinderella had of dancing at a ball and a happily ever after future. I realized that this wishful dream must be important to a woman who was now confined to a wheelchair. The balance of Brother Harold's treatment for Debbie that day was unremarkable.

Two days later, we visited Debbie again. This time, I wondered what I would encounter. I soon found out when a sneaker kept appearing in my vision. Perhaps tennis or simply running was on her mind. I was touched by her fierce determination to beat this illness. I slowly realized that, while Brother Harold was making some progress with her illness, it had developed to the point where a cure was no longer available.

Our third visit to Debbie did not produce shoes in my vision, but this time a pair of sunglasses! The sun does shine quite a bit in California and apparently Paula was hoping to go out and enjoy the brilliant sunshine more.

I started to pay attention to what Brother Harold was doing. He was looking over her body, which appeared in a pancake form. I noticed that there was a hole in the center. It looked like a small bomb had gone off, tearing part of the body apart! I looked a little closer when a small, well designed, metal robot-like device came through the hole and started toward me.

As it came closer, it started shooting energy shots at me! Immediately, I called for my Native American, Two Feathers, to set up more shields and to attack the robot. As he quickly put shields in place, the robot started going out of my view. I told Two Feathers to shoot back at the robot, and to keep shooting until it was dead.

I could not believe what had happened! I had been told to be careful and to take a Native American with me for protection so that I would avoid getting the illness we were treating or becoming too worn down by losing excessive energy. No one had ever mentioned that I needed to watch out for robots that took shots at you! I was stunned.

Two Feathers was firing back, and doing so with fierce passion! The robot had stopped shooting, but Two Feathers continued until it was a pile of burned out essence, which smoldered slightly. I congratulated my guard on a job well done. I was uninjured, and I asked each of my party if they were alright. Relief washed over me when the answer was affirmative.

52

Every day there are always new lessons to be learned. Today, I learned the value of the shields that we used, and promised myself that we would use more of them. I learned that Two Feathers was an experienced warrior during our first combat, and I promised myself that I would be more watchful in the future.

A robot that looked like it was made in Japan? Unbelievable news, and only in California could this happen!

Fibromyalgia is an immune system disease in which the body attacks itself. When the disease has been active for many years, it is obvious that it can develop new weapons to use in its quest to destroy its host. Apparently, it thought I was the enemy and as a result, it tried to destroy me.

The disease was correct – I WAS its enemy. What I found amazing was that the disease had the intelligence to react to new information so quickly and accurately, and that it was capable of building such a robot. Fibromyalgia is not a common disease! I wonder whether it has made other similar robots, or other tools to use against its enemies. These are all frightening thoughts!

Fibromyalgia as a disease definitely requires more study. I fervently hope that one day someone will read this and will have the ability to conduct some meaningful research towards its cure. Until that day in the future arrives, in my own small way, I will continue to study and battle this devastating illness.

CHAPTER 14 – MATT'S ACCIDENT

One day I received a frantic call from a close friend about a family emergency. Matt, a man in his mid-twenties and my friend's son, had been involved in a serious motor vehicle accident. A large dump truck had run into the side of the van that Matt had been driving, critically injuring him!

He had been rushed to the hospital and after some tense medical assessments, the doctors announced with relief to the family that Matt was expected to live. Unfortunately, the bad news was that his left leg might need to be amputated above his knee. Matt's knee was destroyed! All of his ligaments, cartilage, nerves and muscles were severely damaged. The bones below his knee had been almost scraped clean in the aftermath of the collision. This was a terrible accident for this young man!

Immediately, Brother Harold and I rushed to the hospital. Matt was surrounded by nurses and doctors. The only meaningful thing Brother Harold could do was to send healing energy to his leg that was getting so much medical attention. No one in the room could see Brother Harold. Perhaps they could see that his muscles, nerves and tendons started to look healthier, and were responding to treatment quicker. Those changes would be the only visible responses to anyone that improvements were taking place. All these signs are signs that someone is doing something right, or a spirit is practicing spirit techniques to the few who might be aware of the activity taking place. We left, knowing that we would be back later to treat Matt again.

Hours later at five o'clock in the morning, we returned to Matt. He was sleeping peacefully with no one around him. Brother Harold immediately went to his left leg, going underneath the large wrappings that surrounded it. He studied various parts of Matt's leg and encased his leg in powerful healing energy for the next ten minutes. There was little that he could do other than to facilitate its healing and encourage growth in the injured nerves and muscles. This would be a long process of healing for Matt with many visits from Brother Harold.

Part of each visit would include monitoring Matt's attitude and emotions. Accepting such a dramatic change in his life and body would be quite hard for him. He had a new wife as well as a devoted mother and father, all of whom were advantages in such a serious situation. During each of our visits, a complete physical took place, which usually showed nothing new other than some sore muscles. All of Matt's various sore muscles were treated with healing energy.

We continued our morning visits for another week. Matt was healing well, but is would be a long period of time before he would be able to do anything with his injured leg. He was sent home to continue to recuperate and he was encouraged to attend therapy sessions several times each week as his muscles healed and regained their strength.

Over time, our visits dropped to once per week and Brother Harold was pleased with his progress. This continued for another three months. At that point, Brother Harold felt we could reduce our visits to once monthly, barring any future difficulties.

At that point in time, Matt could move around reasonably well, by using crutches or a wheel chair. As we monitored his progress, his attitude showed that he was adjusting well, able to accept new conditions as they occurred. Nothing more could be expected considering how grave this accident had been.

CHAPTER 15 – TERMINAL MAX

Sometimes I sit here in my comfortable chair musing about life in general, and it occurs to me that we sometimes need to contemplate our life. Yes, we deliberate and review, but of what? What it is that takes place in our daily life, reflections of the choices we made, assessments of the outcome of those choices, reviewing our responses, and thoughts about how we might best modify our reactions the next time.

With Brother Harold now a significant part of my life, I have found that many unique experiences occur daily. I stay in a constant state of wonder, which has been the most enjoyable state of living I have ever experienced. Knowing this, I need to comment on several things.

During the past year, I have dealt with several patients who have been labeled "Terminal". "Terminal" simply means that a patient is expected to pass from the physical plane of life within a short period of time, usually in a matter of days, weeks or months. Generally, hospice becomes involved to assist with and manage end of life care for the patient as well as providing familial support.

I do not have a problem with the concept of labeling a seriously ill patient "Terminal". I thoroughly respect the nurses and licensed assistants who are sent from the hospice agencies, the caring and often heart wrenching work they perform. Hospice care is needed and often vitally important to the patient and their families. The hospice team performs a great service to many people. The oncologists I have encountered are also excellent doctors. Every single one that I have met has been a wonderful and caring person.

Since I am a person who deals with spirit medicine, there are some important changes I would propose. I would like Brother Harold to be given the chance to assist oncologists before the cancer patient reaches the terminal stage of their illness.

Why? I believe in Brother Harold's ability to help heal sick patients. I do not wish to share in or take any credit for his successes, but strive to help heal people and return them to their lives successfully. Once a patient has been labeled terminal, and hospice has become involved, seldom is thought given to researching alternative treatments for this patient. While Brother Harold often defeats cancerous growths completely, it is almost impossible to get the patient off morphine and back into a normal and functioning life.

Max was a patient who lived in Wilmington, North Carolina. He had been diagnosed with cancer of the kidney which had spread to his lungs and liver. Max's cancer had been defined as terminal and hospice became involved, which was now providing support for Max and his family. The small church that Max attended was also assisting, sending people to visit him daily. The hospice agency was making sure that he had enough morphine for pain relief, and that he was taking it appropriately. Max spent almost all his time in one room of his apartment, sleeping, eating, watching TV and taking morphine.

Within the first week of treating Max, Brother Harold had cured him of cancer. No cancer, ergo no pain, and no perceived need for morphine. I spoke to Max on the phone and described to him what

Brother Harold had done. After explaining to him why it was important to taper off the morphine he had been taking, he had an interesting response. He believed that he might be addicted to it, which I fully agreed with since it is well known that morphine is a highly addictive prescription medication.

My recommendation was that he should gradually decrease the amount of morphine he was taking on a daily basis until his next oncologist appointment. I suggested that Max receive additional tests to gauge the cancer's progress. Once it became obvious he had no further signs of cancer, he could then ask for help weaning off morphine. Over the next few days Max and I talked several times and I reached an agreement with him. He made an appointment with his oncologist to discuss his condition.

In spite of my assurances that the cancer had been destroyed, there was a lot of pressure placed on Max to continue to take his morphine. Max was continually visited by the staff providing hospice care and parishioners from his church. Whether he told any of them about Brother Harold and the fact that he was cured of cancer, I have no idea. I suspect that if he had, chances were good that he was not believed, and his ravings would have been attributed to morphine addiction. My frustration mounted as I waited for Max's appointment with his oncologist.

Unfortunately, his addiction quickly reached the point where Max could no longer remember if he had taken his morphine or not. Sadly, one day he obviously had forgotten that he had already taken his morphine dose, and he took a repeat dose of his medication. He was later found comatose on the floor in the solitary room he lived in. Because he had fallen, his head had apparently hit the floor in his room quite hard, which caused a concussion and knocked him unconscious.

Sadly, Max never regained consciousness and was dead within two days.

CHAPTER 16 – THE CPA

One Tuesday morning, I went to visit my accountant who was unfamiliar with Brother Harold and the work I performed with him. Sometimes, I do enjoy shocking some people with my story!

Ted has probably heard almost every unusual tale from his clients. He sat stoically looking at me while I patiently took him through my saga. Ted, however, was obviously not bored, and he did not disbelieve me as my cardiologist did. He simply wondered if I was telling him the whole and complete truth. Ted is an intelligent man, and most likely due to our twenty year relationship, was tolerant and knew that I was not a raving lunatic!

After I finished, he sat silently while he looked at me. Finally Ted spoke, and he related to me a story about a friend and the unearthly things he had been going through. Amazingly, I have found that almost everyone has had some experience with the spirit world – whether they were consciously aware of it or not.

He ended by sharing his own health concerns with me. Ted explained that he had one functioning kidney, which worried him a great deal because he was diabetic. His most bothersome problem was a shoulder joint which often became "unhooked" where the ball and socket would move out of position and caused him a bit of pain! He also had a back problem which would trouble him if he needed to remain standing for any length of time, such as during church services.

I promised to look into both concerns with Brother Harold. Five o'clock the next morning came quickly and we visited Ted.

Personally, I have had the same two concerns, so I was quite interested to see how Brother Harold would approach Ted's problems.

First, we tended to his shoulder. Brother Harold placed two replacement strips of tendon over the ball and socket joint in Ted's shoulder, then screwed each end into place. This fix took approximately three quick minutes.

Secondly, we went to Ted's back, where Brother Harold started by looking very closely at each vertebrae and disc in his spine. Brother Harold discovered that two of the vertebra required adjusting and follow up treatment to help them stay in place. The muscles on both sides of the spinal column also needed some treatment. Strangely, I felt as if I were back in the chiropractor's office again!

As Brother Harold finished treating Ted's spine, he very carefully looked over Ted's spine again to be sure no changes had occurred. Ted's shoulder had only taken three minutes, but his spine adjustment took up the remainder of the half hour that we spent with him.

During the next two days we went back to see Ted, each time spending about fifteen minutes checking Ted's spine and applying treatments to it. Brother Harold was doing a much better job than my old chiropractor! Ted's spine was staying in place since he'd received the first adjustment.

A few days later I went back to Ted's office to reclaim my completed tax return. I asked him how he was feeling. Ted smiled quickly. He started rotating his shoulder and triumphantly announced that it was completely fixed! He also told me that he needed to go to a funeral and was worried that he would not be able to stand up as long as he would need. Later, Ted let me know that the funeral went as long as he expected, however he had experienced no discomfort in his spine.

Ted exclaimed "Brother Harold has treated me well!"

I asked Ted to call me if we were ever needed. A new tax year approaches, and Ted has stayed healthy. I am absolutely certain that Ted is thankful that he no longer needs to worry about losing his ability to do his job.

CHAPTER 17 – WIFE NUMBER TWO

My own personal first battle with the ravages of cancer began in 2000 when my wife was diagnosed with breast cancer. Truly, it is one of the most heart-wrenching experiences a man can go through, suffering for and with the person he loves dearly. The stress and difficulties of dealing with cancer in one's wife definitely ranks up there with the death of one's parents.

My wife Clarissa and I went to every single appointment with her doctors together. We planned her surgery together. Sitting in the waiting room for nearly seven and a half hours while Clarissa's operation took place was especially nerve-racking for me. I knew that one breast would be removed and a "tummy tuck" operation would be performed. This operation would allow the plastic surgeon that specialized in breast reconstruction to take enough muscle as well as fat from her lower abdomen area and transplant it to her breast area, creating a new breast to replace the cancerous one.

I suppose, if one looks at the bright side of things, perhaps she would be losing a breast but she would be gaining as well. A slimmer stomach and a new breast were not too bad of a trade off to remove a cancerous breast, or so we thought.

After Clarissa recuperated from her long operation, she faced chemotherapy treatments. Chemotherapy was a horrifying experience which changed my way of thinking. On a regular basis we went to the hospital so that Clarissa could be given tests. These tests basically determined how much chemotherapy i.e., poison, they would give my wife without killing her. Afterwards, there were more blood tests at the oncologist's office. These tests, given before each of her eight rounds of chemotherapy, were to ensure that she was strong and healthy enough to tolerate them. Once the all-ok signal was given, I sat beside Clarissa while she spent two tedious hours receiving the poison drop by drop.

One day, as I waited in the reception area for my wife to return from her latest blood test, my mind wandered. I wondered about some things, and thought to myself, "What a large room this was, filled with patients being poisoned for the sake of a cure. What a large waiting room this was, filled to the brim with patients waiting for their test results. How does a patient handle the news that their blood counts are too low to get their treatment that day?" What I found surprising was just how many patients received test results showing that they were too ill to receive treatment that day.

The nurses, who were the nicest people in the world, showed a great deal of strain on their faces. I wondered if this was because they were incredibly stressed from years of poisoning other people while trying to help them. How sad this all seemed to me, a very deep and dark sadness.

I remember sitting alone in this waiting room at the oncologist's office. I watched the faces of all the patients who faced their own private cancer battles. Somehow, I knew that this scene would someday be part of a book or a movie. What struck me at that moment was how the story of people who faced the enormity of cancer, chemotherapy and its effects on their lives needed to be told to be fully appreciated by others. Unfortunately, I had not met Brother Harold by 2000. He would have been incredibly helpful with these patients, working to cure their cancer and lessening the side effects of chemotherapy.

The first four rounds of chemotherapy that Clarissa faced were the worst. Each round was administered on a Friday, each exactly three weeks apart. Through trial and error, we discovered that Clarissa did far better if she came home and went to bed about three hours later. Clarissa would nap throughout the weekend and wake up periodically to drink water, hot tea, and milkshakes, all "wet" items. The morning after her treatment, she usually had a gravy biscuit, which again, was food that was "wet". One of the side effects that Clarissa suffered as a result of her chemotherapy was a dry mouth, and "wet" food helped to relieve the severe cotton mouth that she had to cope with. By Sunday, she was able to move around a bit and prepare herself for her return to work on Monday.

In comparison, the second four rounds of chemotherapy were "a walk in the park". The drugs used in this particular chemotherapy made the patient's bones hurt, not the joints, but the bones. The medication my wife was directed to take the night before her treatment would make her feel very hyperactive. She would come home post-treatment and remain awake for eighteen to twenty four hours afterwards. Sunday nights she slept on a normal sleep cycle, and Clarissa returned to work on Monday.

I do believe that while the cancer patient has the greater ordeal throughout the whole process, the patient's spouse finishes a strong second. Clarissa and I certainly fit that statement!

After the eighth and final round of chemotherapy, we celebrated as if it were graduation day. The protocol nurse even came around to present Clarissa with a "diploma" for finishing all eight sessions of her chemotherapy. There was a lot of happiness all around us! As we walked out of that depressing clinic for the last time, I looked around the waiting room at all of the new faces that had just arrived. Since I knew what they faced, my heart went out to them.

Radiation treatments followed the chemotherapy treatments. Five tiny dots were tattooed across my wife's "new" breast to precisely mark the area which would receive radiation. Normally, thirty six radiation sessions were prescribed. Clarissa was fortunate, she would only require twenty eight sessions. For nearly six weeks, every weekday morning she woke bright and early and departed for her treatment. Afterwards, she went on to work. Fortunately, she seemed to have no problems with the radiation treatments. Clarissa was an unbelievably strong person who never complained!

Five and one half years later, Clarissa is just finishing up a five year treatment plan with Tamoxifen. After this, she will be taking a different medication for five more years. This medication treatment will be a real walk in the park because we now have Brother Harold to help us!

Ten months ago, I asked Brother Harold to look her over. I explained about the breast cancer she had experienced. Brother

Harold gave her a very thorough examination, which lasted almost an hour. His prognosis for Clarissa?

This time he spoke to me and stated, "She's as healthy as an ox!"

This was certainly a new phrase to me! Perhaps this expression dates back to the period of time when Brother Harold was last on earth in a physical form. This must be from back in the olden days when oxen were plentiful and valued as farm animals.

CHAPTER 18 – THE ONCOLOGIST

My first battle with cancer set up my second battle. My wife's oncologist, Stan, was a hand selected man who has an excellent reputation and a wonderful bedside manner. I was in my wife's hospital room one day when he entered the room. He walked up to me and introduced himself. "Hi, my name is Stan," he said as he shook my hand before walking over to Clarissa to shake hers. He then sat next to her on the bed, took out a pad of paper and started talking and writing notes at the same time.

I sat down next to him, completely amazed at his friendliness as well as his authority and knowledge. Clarissa and I were both new to the world of cancer, and he explained all of the procedures that we could expect to happen to us. He continued to write lengthy notes as he spoke. Half an hour later, we had gained a lot of new knowledge, had asked many questions, and he had gotten to know us. After we finished our conversation, he stood up, shook our hands again, and handed the pad full of writing to my wife, saying to her "This is what we talked about, and you can refer back to these notes whenever you need to."

What a nice, personable and intelligent man he was!

Four years later, after I had begun working with Brother Harold, my wife had an appointment with Stan for her normal follow-up exam. I went along with her to the appointment, thinking that I would explain Brother Harold to him. My plan was to ask him if there were some patients I could try to help.

As I thought about the approach I would use with him, I remembered the first meeting we had in the hospital four years ago. I decided that I would borrow his method and type up some notes about Brother Harold, with the intent of sharing them with him. He could digest them quickly and be up to speed.

With some editing and revisions, I boiled my notes down to one page, and we went to see Stan. I waited until after Clarissa's examination was over and we sat together, simply talking. I handed my typewritten sheet to him, and he read over my notes within a few seconds. After he thought things over for a few moments, he commented to me that he found this subject quite interesting! I explained to Stan that I wanted to help the patients in any way possible, without interfering with his practice.

Mentally, he debated the pros and cons for a few minutes, and then Stan suggested that he could give me the names of three patients, all of whom were deemed "Terminal." They all had a prognosis of two weeks or less to survive, would I be interested in seeing what I could do to help them?

"I would appreciate the opportunity!" I exclaimed.

He smiled, "I suggest that you act quickly, because they are definitely on their way out."

Clarissa and I immediately went home. I summoned Brother Harold, Two Feathers and Dr. Price, then began by introducing my group of patients and the time limitations that we had with these three terminally ill patients. Our patients were David, Mary and Paul. I chose to begin with David.

74

My initial impression of David was that he was very tired of battling his illness, and I intuitively realized that he was very close to being ready to let go. I encouraged him to give us a chance to reverse the course of his illness. When Brother Harold scanned his body, I saw no black seeds, but I did see some active cancer which he eliminated immediately. Once all the cancer had been removed, and all of David's organs had been checked, Brother Harold gave him many healing rays of energy. By giving him some of our energy, our thoughts were that David would continue to draw on those energy reserves to give him more strength and courage to continue his valiant fight.

Mary was our next patient. She was in dreadful condition! She did have energy with her as we examined Mary, but every time she coughed, parts of her energy drifted away. I had never seen this happen before! As Brother Harold scanned Mary, we saw many of those terrible black seeds. The first thing Brother Harold did was to destroy all of the seeds, and then he went back over her body and eliminated the rest of her active cancer cells. Finally, we bathed her body with healing energy rays. Throughout this entire session, Mary continued her coughing. I could see how she would constantly lose bits of energy each time her chest shook with those deep coughs! We were with Mary for forty five minutes and I was relieved when we were done with our session. The doctor was right. We had been given the worst and most hopeless terminal cases.

Paul was the last patient that we visited. As I viewed his energy, my depression continued. I sat there and felt numb as I watched an almost dead man who existed with almost no energy left. Paul was slowly wasting away with almost no desire to continue living. Brother Harold felt the same as I did. We stayed with Paul for half an hour, doing nothing except to give him soothing and comforting energy, which is the only way to describe our ministrations. Even though we accomplished nothing more beyond giving Paul comfort, it was a good feeling for me. I knew that sometimes, when a person is at the end of his life span, often all that is needed is to provide them with a blanket of comfort and love.

This day had been an extremely difficult one for me. I knew that my energy had been drained to a precariously low level as I had visited David, Mary and Paul. I realized that I needed to discuss with Dr. Price how to control the use of my energy, making sure it was kept at safe levels while I funneled it to Brother Harold as he worked to help our patients. Visiting these three people today had used quite a bit of my energy reserves!

Over the next two weeks, we visited Mary and David daily. Brother Harold and I discussed what to do with Paul, and we decided that Paul would receive one comfort visit from us per week as long as he remained with us. There was no point to prolonging the inevitable conclusion to his battle.

During our visits to David, I realized that he had made a life based on his interest in music. He had reached the point where he no longer had the strength to perform with his instrument, and felt that life had lost all of its meaning. I told David that I could feel the piece of music that continued to play through his mind. It was a composition that he

76

had never put on paper. It would be forever lost if he did not write it down for the world to enjoy! I tried to give him a reason to continue living, and encouraged him to complete one last task before he died. Whether he put this composition to paper, I will never know. I hope for his sake that he did.

My fourth visit to Mary was meaningful to me. By the time we made our third visit to her, Mary's coughing had stopped! As we began our fourth session, a woman suddenly ran up to me as I watched Brother Harold perform his work. She stopped in front of me and said, "Thank you so much!" and began to hug me.

This was a truly unique experience! I am not sure exactly what part of me travels with Brother Harold, but I know that that part of me can communicate, has vision and provides energy. What I understood was that a younger version of an old woman came running up to whatever part of me that was there, and threw her arms around me thanking me from the bottom of her heart. When I think back on this moment, I am moved by it all over again. I did not get to know Mary very well, but I did sense the strength of her religious convictions and how important a part of her life they were. I am pleased that I was able to provide some comfort to her.

Nine weeks later, I received my single phone call from Stan to tell me that all three patients had passed away. I do not know how much longer Paul had lived, but I do know that David and Mary had extended their lives far beyond the initial two week prognosis that I had been given. Assuredly, there was no cancer that remained in their bodies, and I know that they lived happier, healthier lives until they passed away after my first visit to them. Brother Harold and I were happy about our results!

CHAPTER 19 – TRAVELING THE OPTIC NERVE

Nine years ago I met a manicurist, May, who was married to the owner of an electrical company. She was an extremely attractive woman, close to my age, and was happily married to her second husband. My wife and I regularly visited May at the manicurist salon, and she did excellent work. As we got to know her, we all became very good friends.

When May's second marriage ended in divorce, her life became quite difficult. She was devastated when it finalized, and turned to alcohol as a means of comfort. Unfortunately, the problems that she created for herself affected our friendship to a certain degree. We continued our weekly appointments with May, and in doing so, remained aware of all of her difficulties.

At one point, I had mentioned that I belonged to the Mensa Association, and she had decided from that knowledge that she knew the smartest person in town. As a result, this led to being asked for advice on numerous personal decisions she had to make. In spite of all these challenges, I still liked her.

May was connected to the spirit world through her deceased mother, an Indian guide, and a playful child who continually played tricks on her. She had very good intuitive abilities which probably kept her out of trouble a fair number of times. Ultimately, her intuition led her back to her former husband, which resulted in a reconnection between the two of them that lasted for many years.

Once May retired from the nail salon business, we lost touch with each other for a few months. Out of the blue one day, she contacted me through my email on my computer, asking me for a recommendation of a good neurologist in town. I sent her the name of one that I knew, and then asked May what was bothering her.

"I am having a lot of pain with headaches, and I can't see out of my left eye! I went to my eye doctor and he suggested that I see a neurologist," was her answer. I told her that the neurologist I recommended was a competent one.

"Perhaps Brother Harold might be able to help you." I also suggested.

May told me at this point that she would try anything to relieve her pain! I asked her to lie down and try to relax, and our spirits would be there momentarily to see what we could do.

I sat down, gathered my troops, and we were off. First, Brother Harold went straight to her good eye. After he examined it from the outside, we traveled to the optic nerve in the middle of the eye, and moved down its length, directly into the brain. The optic nerve appeared as a white string as we traveled to its end, toward the back of the brain where it is attached.

After we looked this nerve over, we jumped over to May's other eye, and started from where the optic nerve began and traveled on it as we again headed towards her brain. This time, when we arrived in the brain, I noticed that something was very different. This nerve seemed not to be nearly as tight, and appeared to be firing off sight signals into the brain at random! There were lines of signals that had not been

80

completed, and were not understood by her brain. These sight signals were simply drifting off aimlessly into the surface of brain matter which controlled other functions in her body. This was what apparently had created the unusual pain that she had been feeling!

In hindsight, I assumed that Brother Harold must have grabbed the optic nerve, because we continued traveling as we had with the first optic nerve. Finally, we circled around to where the detached nerve belonged. Brother Harold efficiently and quickly reattached May's optic nerve.

In a flash we were out, and at this point I knew that our job was done. Afterwards, I realized that May must have been hit in the head very hard to detach such a nerve. Intuitively, I somehow knew that her husband was responsible for ending one particularly bad fight in that way.

Not knowing May's telephone number, I waited to hear from her. It took several days, but I finally found her on line and asked how she was doing.

"I don't know what you did, but keep it up! My eyesight came back and my headaches are gone, and it happened minutes after we talked online a few days ago," May said excitedly!

I explained to May what Brother Harold had done. Sometimes, it is quite difficult to explain to a person that you and three other spirits had been in their brain! I honestly do not know whether she believed my explanation or not. I suspect that part of her probably wrote it off as a natural occurrence with no assistance from me, and another part of her told her that what I said was true. I felt her conflicted emotions, but could only wish her well.

Unfortunately, we have since lost touch with each other, and no longer communicate. I cannot say how she has progressed after Brother Harold and I assisted her.

CHAPTER 20 – ANNA, THE MOTHER-IN-LAW

Before we divorced in 1992, I was married to my first wife, Susan, for twenty three years. During our marriage, we raised two sons who are now happily married, and are raising wonderful children of their own.

Susan's parents, my in-laws, lived in Anderson, South Carolina, which is a small southern town. Since I grew up and resided in New York City until I was eighteen, prior to attending Randolph-Macon College in Virginia, I was considered very much a "northerner". The first time I met my future wife's paternal grandmother, proved to be quite an interesting occasion. I was warned repeatedly by Susan and her mother, Anna, to be careful while addressing her grandmother, Emma. She did not like "Yankees", and may not be polite, they warned! Her son, Walter Sr. who was Susan's father, remained silent.

Emma had been married to a gentleman who was southern born and bred, and had fought with the confederate army during the Civil War. Unfortunately, he met his demise during the War which resulted in lifelong feelings of resentment by my wife's grandmother against the "Yankee so and so's" who had murdered him. After getting to know Emma, I admit in all fairness she was a very gentle, decent and honorable southern woman who I came to greatly admire before she passed away.

The greatest challenge I faced during my first marriage was my relationship with my mother-in-law, Anna. Prior to our marriage, my wife lived in Richmond in a shared apartment with other college students. At that time, we were seeing each other frequently and I often visited Susan in Richmond. I had kept a bottle of bourbon at my girlfriend's apartment for our future use. Imagine my dismay when we discovered on one of Anna's visits to her daughter, she had helped herself to and emptied a half-full quart sized bottle of bourbon. Since I was a college student as well and not very flush with funds, this was a sign to me of pending difficulties in my relationship with my future mother-in-law.

Unfortunately, there was a lot of friction and arguments between Anna and me, which resulted in a year of silence between us. The unexpected death of Susan's brother, Walter Jr., in a plane crash ended the silence and resulted in an unavoidable reconciliation.

Anna had lost her son, Walter, Jr., in that tragic accident of the small plane. This had made that year's Christmas holiday a terribly sad holiday for the entire family. Walter, Jr., as well as his brother-in-law, father-in-law, and close friend, had all perished in the plane crash while they were traveling to pick up a new kitten meant to be a Christmas present. Susan and I drove to South Carolina in temperatures which hovered around one degree that Christmas day to pay our respects and to attend the funeral two days later.

Shortly after the funeral, Anna and Walter Sr. moved into an apartment in a church supported retirement home. They lived there until 2003, when Walter Sr. passed away. Losing her husband, Walter Sr., brought back memories of the terrible accident in which her son was killed.

A few months after Walter's death, during one Wednesday meeting at my house, the Development Circle was told by a spirit that there were forty people, mostly victims of plane crashes to see someone. I assumed some of those victims might include my brother-in-law, his father-in-law, and the other men who had died years ago in that Christmas Eve plane crash. It turned out to be those four and thirty some other spirits who had heard that there were a number of plane crash victims going to a meeting on earth. They, having all perished in plane crashes, decided to attend also. It is sometimes difficult on a spiritual level to make sense of such tragic things when they happen.

After I asked the crowd if Walter, Sr., Susan's father, was present, a spirit right in front of me started to bounce! I then greeted him and asked if Walter, Jr., was present. Right then, another spirit started bouncing as well! I was very pleased that I had both Walters in front of me. A lot of problems were settled emotionally for me that night, leaving only gratitude and good wishes for these spirits. I experienced the sadness that Walter, Sr. had felt when he lost his son. He had been totally devastated. He was never himself after that sad event. To see Walter Sr. and his son together again felt wonderful. They had both been genuinely nice men, lived good lives, and would spend a fine eternity together.

I heard through my sons that their grandmother, Anna, was not a happy woman. She had suffered through breast cancer and was a cancer survivor physically, but psychologically had not coped with the rigors of cancer treatment very well. My opinion was that she missed

85

having her husband to wait on her hand and foot, and felt that joining him in an afterlife might bring about the return of his servitude.

After several days of soul searching, I decided to go with Brother Harold to investigate what we could do to help this sad woman. In April of 2005, we arrived at Anna's side energetically one morning and began our work. As Brother Harold surveyed her energy, I was shocked to see how flimsy it had become. As Brother Harold normally does, he "flattened" the spirit energy of her body into a fried egg-like object. He began to study the white portion of her energy. Instead of being firm, her white portion appeared as if it were torn tissue paper. As I watched, a terrible feeling of giving up came over me, which I realized were Anna's emotions! I immediately started to work with the "tissue paper" portion by pulling its pieces together. It was an almost unbelievably difficult task, but one I was determined to accomplish while Brother Harold worked to re-invigorate her organs. After we worked for nearly an hour, I was beginning to feel exhausted. I received a message from Dr. Price, the chemist, who informed me that it was time for us to leave. As we left, her spirit energy, which had appeared as the fried egg object, looked much more life-like. The overwhelming feeling of despair and giving up I had been sensing were gone. I felt that things were back in order as we left.

Drained, I slept for four hours. Afterwards, I woke up and felt as if I had been in a boxing match and lost badly. This feeling of exhaustion remained with me for two days in spite of sleeping for several additional hours during this time.

For the entire year that I had been working with Brother Harold, this was the toughest and most difficult physical aftereffect response I had faced. For all the energy healing sessions that have been held since our visit to Anna, I increased the standard number of shields that Two Feathers put up between me and the patient. I promised myself that I would avoid draining myself to this degree in healing sessions, and to protect myself as much as possible from such intensely upsetting emotional issues from the patients in the future.

CHAPTER 21 – THE RETIRED COUPLE

Many years ago, I was raised by a family that was not very active in religious circles. My grandmother was a firm believer in organized religion, and raised her daughter, my mother, to follow its structured rules. Since my father was 52 years old when I was born, we did not have a particularly close relationship and I never knew what spiritual belief structure my father was brought up with. While growing up in New York City, I was exposed to many different churches and other religious sanctuaries. I suspect that my parent's ulterior motive was to keep me busy on Sundays!

Recently, I began to work with some clients who are now in their eighties, and doing quite well. This particular couple had their own apartment in a Baptist affiliated retirement center. Every day, they took two of their meals in the dining hall. If they needed medical assistance, there was nearby medical help. Their apartment boasted two bedrooms, a living room and kitchen and was situated in a large multi-story building with an elevator. The grounds were professionally maintained.

Ralph had had a successful bypass heart operation fifteen years ago. A few months ago, he began to have some problems that alarmed his cardiologist. At his age, with one bypass operation already completed, his future was looking a little shaky.

I knew Ralph's children, who approached me with their worries. Ralph and his wife had no place for the spirit world in their belief system. This type of spirituality was contrary to everything that their church had taught them, and in the wife's beliefs, would be considered to be verging on satanic. Of their three children, one was a minister and another was married to a minister. Both of these children were familiar with Brother Harold's healing work on a first hand basis, and knew that he was most definitely not satanic! They felt, and I agreed, that Brother Harold might be able to provide some helpful treatment for their parents.

Initially, we decided to work on Ralph first. At 5:00 the next morning, I briefly updated Brother Harold on Ralph's condition. As is usual with new patients, I waited for two or three minutes before we started. Truthfully, I have no idea why there is a delay before Brother Harold and I begin, but I jokingly suggested to him that he was checking his big book before we started the job!

Once we arrived, Brother Harold started by completely surveying Ralph's physical condition. Finally, he reached and studied his heart. I could see the big jumble of arteries which was the result of Ralph's previous surgery. Heart bypass operations usually make a mess of the supply lines to the heart by replacing and grafting in new lines. Sometimes one might hear of a second bypass operation, but very seldom will a third bypass be performed.

Brother Harold began by creating a substitute heart. He replaced one of the valves, and reduced the size of the heart substantially, which allowed it to beat more efficiently. Once Brother Harold sewed it together, he replaced the current heart. Brother Harold then watched as it commenced beating to make sure no unpleasant surprises cropped up. He inspected Ralph's heart beat for a longer period than I expected he might have. Obviously, Brother Harold was not pleased with how it was functioning. Suddenly, he started over again with another replacement heart!

I watched carefully, earnestly hoping I was not watching his first failure in an 86 year old patient! After a few minutes, Brother Harold finished, replaced the second heart, and watched carefully. This time, within three or four minutes, our spiritual surgeon was satisfied with his results. I exhaled a long breath.

When Ralph woke up that morning, he felt better than usual! It was going to be a good day, he thought. His children were more attentive than they normally were which pleased him. Ralph, feeling far more invigorated than he had been for quite some time, was in for many more happy years!

Sally, Ralph's wife, was our next patient. The following morning, we traveled to his wife. This time, I noticed the same thin, torn paper-like appearance to her energy, similar to but not nearly as critically thin as my mother-in-law's energy had been. Again I felt similar feelings of desperation from her, but this time I started talking to Sally then gave her many inspirational and supportive words. I began to repair the tears in her tissue-like energy. This time, I had a sense of gratefulness and relief from Sally. I continued until I felt that her energy was whole again. Afterwards, I felt well overall and not nearly as worn out as I had been after working on my mother-in-law. This time, my job was far easier, and I was glad that I could make a difference for Sally.

It has been ten months since Brother Harold and I visited this charming couple, and I am glad to report that Ralph and Sally are both doing extremely well!

CHAPTER 22 – JANE AND JOHN

Jane was a friend of mine who I had met on the computer in a cooking chat room. We both had experience in real estate, and our friendship started based on our common interests. She was married and the proud parent of five wonderful children who ranged in age from a four year old child to a freshman in college. Jane was also an ardent Catholic.

One Saturday morning, after Jane and I had known each other online for about a year, her husband had woken up and gone outside with the intention of mowing the grass. A scant hour later, John came inside and poured himself a glass of water. After taking a quick drink, he stopped, turned to his wife and told her that he wasn't feeling well. A strange look rapidly came over his face and he told her that he thought he was in trouble. Suddenly, he collapsed onto the floor, dying instantly of a massive coronary.

At John's funeral, I met Jane. Fortunately, her husband left her well taken care of with adequate amounts of insurance. After the dust settled following his funeral, Jane decided to move back to her home state of Pennsylvania. Before Jane departed, I had a chance to talk to her on the phone. She was very aware of my interest in metaphysics and asked me if I could send a message to John. I said I could certainly try to do that, but he may be unable to reply yet, or I may not even receive a reply. Jane's message was short and succinct, "Tell him that the children are all okay, I will take good care of them, and I miss him and love him."

I asked Jane for a few minutes before we continued our conversation online. Quietly, I sat with my eyes closed and called out for John. With experience, I have learned to wait patiently before receiving a response, especially if I am seeking a new spirit. After a short period of time, I called him again. After approximately four minutes, I saw a blue energy appear and I realized that John had arrived. Usually, I see very new spirits in yellow, so seeing his blue energy was different!

I had never met John, but as I viewed his energy, I could tell it was the man I had heard so much about. His energy formed two circles, one inside the other, very neatly shaped and equidistant from each other by one inch. They appeared exactly as if someone had been drawing circles with crayons, making absolutely certain that they were staying within the lines. He had been an obsessive/compulsive man on earth while in his physical body, and he is obsessive/compulsive as a spirit! At that moment, I gave him Jane's message. John approached, coming quite close to me, and I wondered if perhaps he was trying to shake my hand! I wished him well, and I headed back.

Afterwards, I explained to Jane how his energy had appeared to me and she was very amused. "Yes, that is John!" she acknowledged. I was glad that I could help maintain a connection between these two special people.

A few months later, Jane connected with me online. She had settled into her new home in Pennsylvania, but was very troubled. She was very concerned about Gilbert, John's father, who was seriously ill in the hospital. He already had two previous heart bypass operations, and was suffering from heart problems again. Unfortunately, this time it appeared that the doctors might not be able to help him. She asked me if Brother Harold could possibly help!

The next morning, we arrived at Gilbert's bedside in Pennsylvania. The menagerie of arteries we found was absolutely amazing. After looking over Gilbert's heart, Brother Harold expertly sized up the situation, created a replacement heart and quickly replaced a valve. It was exchanged with the heart in Gilbert's chest, observed for four minutes before Brother Harold decided he was satisfied, and we left. Gilbert would be okay!

Later, Jane reported that he had been sent home two days after we had visited him, and Gilbert's heart function had vastly improved! It is always a gratifying feeling to know that we are able help others.

CHAPTER 23 – CELIAC DISEASE

One day, I was idly browsing around online. I visited the membership directory for AOL and set up parameters for a search in the North Carolina membership for anyone who had listed "Metaphysics" as an interest. Surprisingly, I got a list of several names! I read several profiles, and sent a variety of messages to the profile summaries that interested me.

As I conversed with a variety of people, I discovered that two of them were patients that were suffering from Celiac Disease. This is an unfamiliar illness to me, but I discovered that it is quite common. Celiac Disease is an autoimmune disease that results from the body's inability to digest gluten in a variety of grains. As a result, the interior walls of the small intestines become coated so that they cannot benefit from normal digestion of food. The result can be serious weight loss from malnutrition. Usually, a strict dietary regimen is required to maintain a healthy weight.

These two women met each other in a support group of people who all shared this disease. I initially had exchanged a letter with Doris, commenting on her metaphysical interests. She introduced me to her friend Terry, who was also a patient living with Celiac Disease. Doris felt that she was managing well with her disease, but she wanted help for her friend. I quickly assured her that we would help both of them.

The next morning, I explained the disease to Brother Harold, but he already seemed to be familiar with it! There was no hesitation on his part when we went to visit Terry. I was curious to see how he would treat her. After we arrived, the first thing I saw was something that appeared to be alive. I realized it was a small piece of energy which appeared as a strange sort of blue matter. We stopped while Brother Harold studied it for two minutes.

Suddenly, he started firing bolts of energy at this blue matter, and continued until it was dead! As I looked around, I saw more little pieces of the same energy that appeared to be children or offshoots from the parent energy. He relentlessly blasted all of these "children" until they were destroyed as well. I think this definitely qualifies as a justifiable case of infanticide! Apparently, we had just annihilated the force that controlled the Celiac Disease in Terry's body.

Brother Harold proceeded to the intestines and started a flow of brown medicine which covered all of Terry's intestines. This dark medicine appeared thin and coated them well. What an interesting first treatment this turned out to be for Terry!

On our second visit, we went directly to the uppermost section of Terry's intestines, and Brother Harold sent groups of yellow light into them. The lights remained lit as they slid down the intestines, and another group was dropped to follow the first batch. I knew that they were healing lights which would illuminate the intestines through its entire length. After thirty or forty groups of yellow healing lights were released, Brother Harold began to drop thicker material into her intestines, also illuminated. Obviously, quite a bit of medication was involved during these treatments! During our third session, the healing yellow light treatments were repeated.

When we saw Doris, he took a different approach. Brother Harold and I had the impression she was doing much better than Terry had been. This time, Brother Harold dropped lighted blue matter into her intestines. I was told that this treatment was not nearly as intensive as Terry's had been.

That next time I spoke to Doris, and she agreed with Brother Harold's assessment. She said that she felt a lot better, and that Terry was finally starting to gain some weight! Terry's weight had dropped to an alarmingly low 100 pounds.

Doris also mentioned that Terry suffered from persistent sinusitis, a problem that never seemed to quite go away. I let Doris know that we could certainly help Terry's sinusitis. I remarked that it would have been helpful if we had known, and asked if she had any other problems that she needed help with! I'm glad for Terry's sake that there were no additional concerns.

Doris also had a chronic bronchial problem which needed to be addressed by Brother Harold. Apparently, whenever we started making progress on one disease, another made its appearance. I knew we had improved their Celiac Disease, and I knew we would be able to handle their sinusitis and bronchial problems. That alone is worth my while, to recognize that we were able to make a difference in the lives of these two kind women.

CHAPTER 24 – ESOPHAGEAL CANCER

Today, this Saturday morning was beautiful. The sun was shining and the temperature was expected to rise into the mid-seventies. I was about to start on my book when I heard my lawnmower start. I immediately realized that Steve, the manager of one of my rental properties, had arrived. Steve is a large African American man who cuts our grass weekly. He genuinely enjoys working, does a great job managing my property, and volunteers to work in my yard as well. I am quite lucky to know him!

An hour later, after he'd completed the yard. I heard him come into the house. I picked up his check and walked into the kitchen and saw Steve. Handing him his check, I asked him to have a seat. He was a little worn out, grateful to sit down to relax, and rubbed his left elbow in the process. Puzzled, I asked him if he was having a problem. Steve mentioned the pain that he was feeling in his elbow, so I asked if I could try to help him. He agreed to let me take a shot at it!

I explained the mechanics of Reiki to him and told him that my hands would start to feel hot. I suggested that he sit still and wait patiently for about six to eight minutes while I sent Reiki energy to his elbow. He gave me a strange look. I did not laugh, but I knew he was thinking about my hands becoming hot, and wondered how strange that would be. I explained to Steve that Reiki was a 2,500 year old Chinese method of healing energy treatment, and that I was trained in its use. As we sat, I could feel the heat start to come into my hands as they held his elbow.

101

While we waited, we talked about energy healing work. Steve told me about an older gentleman that he was working with and who was having a terrible time with esophageal cancer. He was receiving chemotherapy treatment, had a tube placed into his abdomen for daily feeding since he could not take any food orally, and was still employed so that he could feed himself. Compassionately, I asked for the man's name so that Brother Harold and I could help him.

By now, eight minutes had gone by and Steve stood up, flexing his left arm. He grinned and said, "It does feel better!" I grinned too, and I promised to visit his friend, Jeff, the next morning.

At 5:00 am, we were there. I could see very little, but I waited while Brother Harold continued to work on Jeff. After half an hour, with nothing extraordinary to report, I assumed we were finished.

The next morning, we returned. Brother Harold started working, and again I saw nothing. This time, I asked my crew if they could see what was going on. Two Feathers responded by adding four more shields in front of me, reducing the light even further. Suddenly, I saw the fierce battle that was taking place! Brother Harold was using energy bolts to destroy the esophageal cancer cells, which were tiny and almost invisible. We had fought many different cancers, but these were the smallest cells I had ever seen.

Once again, doubt raised its head concerning the events that were or were not taking place. Sternly, I chastised myself for assuming the worst. I promised myself that I would start by assuming the best outcome would result, and then prove the best had occurred.

102

Later, I made a call to Steve to give him a report on our first two visits, and find out if he had heard from Jeff. Steve said that he had not talked to him, but he had seen him walking up the street earlier in the day, and he appeared to be walking better. "He was walking as if he felt a lot better!" Steve again demonstrated to me there are many ways of communicating with others.

CHAPTER 25 – SIMON

One day I received a call from Simon, who was an old friend. He was sixty-five years old now, and we had been friends most of my life. Our comradeship dated back to our days in New York City, before we attended college. I had kept him fully abreast of my activities with Brother Harold. Since he was quite interested in metaphysics as well as endowed by an active ego, he checked "my friend" and myself out, conversing with some high powered people knowledgeable in the spirit field. We passed his evaluations, and he was told by one of his experts that "I am surrounded by spirits who know what they are doing!"

Empowered by this report, I looked forward to his next call. When it came, it regarded a physical problem he was experiencing with his right hand. Simon's thumb, first and second fingers occasionally felt numb and he had no idea why. He was quite concerned and asked me for help. I too was concerned, and promised we would do our best to solve his problem.

Simon had spent his life dedicating himself to become an expert competitor in tennis and squash. While in college, he ranked at the top standings in both sports. He avidly continued to play with the New York Athletic Club after his graduation, and ranked near the top in each sport there as well. Also a businessman, he was quite successful in the corporate world, and Simon participated in both tennis and squash regularly to maintain the energy he needed.

Now, at sixty-five, he was starting to pay for his dedication to excellence in sports. He already had four knee operations, each on the diminishing cartilage that remained. One hip had been replaced, and his other hip was due to be replaced shortly. He limped noticeably as his ball and socket joint were virtually rubbing against each other bone on bone, which can be extremely painful. As his friend, I was glad that he had not chosen football to excel in! NFL retirees have a tendency to fare badly by the time they reach his age.

The next morning, we visited Simon and Brother Harold looked over his entire body. Finally, we went into his right hand and examined the area around his thumb and first two fingers, looking for anything unusual or out of place. Satisfied that nothing was amiss, we located the nerves in those fingers, and followed them up Simon's arm.

We tracked the nerves, examining them for any problems, which turned out to be a very tedious and time consuming process. At one point in his arm, just above the elbow, we encountered a problem with the main nerve. His nerve appeared as if it were a cable with numerous wires inside it, with a torn exterior and exposed interior wires. We briefly stopped while Brother Harold repaired the tear. Apparently, some sort of trauma in the past caused this old injury. After it was repaired, our journey continued.

So far, everything appeared normal. We got to Simon's shoulder, rounded the corner, and continued to travel on the main nerve, moving toward his spine. I suddenly noticed that the covering of the main nerve appeared to be falling off in sheets. It looked as if a rain storm

106

had blown through, which gave the torn covering the appearance of sheets of rain dripping off the nerve! Each of these sheets was hanging in place, as if there were no wind.

Brother Harold immediately went into action and strapped a band, which looked like a metal strip with holes punched into it, around the nerve. Brother Harold folded all the loose sheets back over the nerve and then wrapped the band around it, then fastened it securely. It made a nice, neat package, and guaranteed none of the nerves would be lost!

We ended our trip at the spine where the nerve connected to the spinal cord. At this point, we were finished. We had inspected its full length, made one repair, and encased about a foot of nerve in a band to maintain its integrity. I took off my blindfold, looked at the clock and noticed we had been working for just over an hour! This was a long time for a spirit medicine visit.

Later, I called Simon and we discussed what we had done. Afterwards, I waited patiently to realize how successful we had been, which can be difficult. A few days later, Simon and I talked again. Simon was very pleased since most of his numbness had disappeared.

Still, there were occasional brief flashes of the numbness, but it was vastly improved. Unfortunately, sometimes certain conditions cannot be fixed "as good as new." Ultimately, this meant Simon would need to adjust and learn to live with these moments of numbness. I knew that we would work with Simon in the future on other health problems.

CHAPTER 26 – BLOCKAGE

It was another very early morning! At five a.m., I was scheduled to visit Hillary and MJ. They both had been diagnosed with Fibromyalgia and would be receiving a treatment today. Hillary also had systemic candidia in her blood which was causing problems for her.

Hillary was our first stop. I was quite curious to see what Brother Harold's treatment would be for candidia, which was affecting her system. Apparently, she had already received medication treatments from her local doctors to remove it from her body. After I ran through my initial prayer and called the posse to arms, Brother Harold began his treatment.

He set up a machine and attached it to an artery. Within a matter of a few minutes, Hillary's blood had passed through the machine and removed all of her candidia. This marvelous machine was quickly disconnected, and there was still time to treat her Fibromyalgia! Sometimes, I am reminded how often we forget that simple and straightforward approaches to healing are still the best ways!

When we finished with Hillary's treatments, we traveled to MJ. I suggested to Brother Harold that we treat her aggressively today, perhaps even address her depression problems. As a result, Brother Harold seemed to be working more forcefully than usual, and covered a considerable amount of territory quickly. We continued at this pace for about five minutes until my view abruptly became very dark.

Immediately, I expected the worst! Not surprisingly, the blue energy that we had seen a few days ago quickly materialized. I had thought that Brother Harold had destroyed it that day. Obviously, I was wrong! As I looked closely at our adversary, I saw that it had been damaged and its presence was smaller. It was still alive and definitely required our attention before we could proceed any further.

Brother Harold arrived and started hitting it dead on with damaging energy waves. This time, the energy prepared for each attack by covering and shielding itself with a band of its own blue energy. Brother Harold's wave of yellow energy would attack and chip off the new band of blue energy. Each time a new yellow energy wave approached, bent on inflicting damage, a new band of blue energy would quickly run around to encircle the blue parent energy. Even in a weaker state, this blue energy was still a formidable adversary.

As I watched this scenario play out, I realized that I needed to call Two Feathers to come in and break the tie that was rapidly developing! Two Feathers is a very aggressive Native American, who does not play games. Brother Harold continued to shoot energy waves while Two Feathers mounted a new attack from the rear. This plan of attack was geared to destroy our foe immediately. Thirty seconds later, the battle was over and we were victorious! Now I was absolutely certain that any blue energy which appeared in MJ in the future would be new energy, not old.

I called MJ to give her an update and she enjoyed hearing about our experiences. She happily let me know that she had not felt this

110

well for quite some time, and her depression was lifting. This left me feeling very positive about her progress, and I had a gut feeling that a few more treatment might work wonders. MJ mentioned that her stomach was causing her pain. A year ago, she had experienced bleeding in her stomach, so this new pain concerned me. I asked her to sit down, saying that we would be right over.

Three minutes later we were there. It felt like forever before we arrived because I was so concerned, but it really took only one short minute.

We were blocked.

Brother Harold was pushing hard, but we were really blocked. I suddenly realized with some shock that she had an intestinal blockage, or some type of blockage very close to her stomach. MJ was taking some pills meant to neutralize excess acid in her stomach. She had been working out of doors and bending over caused heartburn, and the excess acid seemed to be backing up towards her throat. Now with the blockage we found, that seemed more probable.

These were the thoughts that passed through my mind while Brother Harold continued with his work. Suddenly, there was movement! The blockage was moving. Somehow, it was being folded up on itself, but more importantly for our patient it was moving. Perhaps Brother Harold had cut it into pieces, but it finally moved out of sight.

Afterwards, I called MJ and asked her how she felt. She remarked that the pain in her abdomen was gone. She could now push on her abdomen with no pain. She pronounced herself cured!

As a preventative measure for MJ, I suggested that she eat a serving of oatmeal with milk every morning to prevent any recurrences. It was not exactly her favorite food, she grumbled, but she agreed.

CHAPTER 27 – SPINE WORK

Simon called again, and mentioned to me how he was having some problems with his spine. He sees a chiropractor several times a week, and has visited this particularly talented man for the past 26 years. At Simon's request, Brother Harold and I paid him a visit to examine his back.

Simon suffers from a degenerating spine that will "go out" seemingly at will. When it's "out", the resulting pain usually requires treatment. His chiropractor often treats unaligned spines by repairing the structure of his spine in a normal earthly manner, but I suspect that he uses some help from the spirit world. Interestingly, this is apparently a different type of help than what Brother Harold provides.

Our first trip began with a study of Simon's body and its energy. Brother Harold decided to create a duplicate spine which he very quickly disassembled into its individual vertebrates. He quickly examined each one as he reassembled the spine, starting from the base. Within two minutes, each vertebra had been studied and carefully placed in order separated by discs. Brother Harold was very vigilant as he placed each one in the correct order, making any small adjustments necessary, until each one was placed exactly where he wanted it.

Finally, Brother Harold gave Simon's spine a quick and careful examination before he gave an approving replacement nod. The duplication was made and his patient was in a lot better shape.

Next, because Brother Harold knew that Simon's spine was a tough case due to its degenerative and debilitating condition, he treated it with a medicated tape. This tape was wrapped around his spine, which was meant to support it and give it strength. The tape would dissolve over a few days, and the medication would be absorbed by the spine, thereby making it stronger and healthier. After the wrapping of the spine was completed, we watched as it performed without trouble.

Afterward, I called Simon to assess his feelings. Over the years, he has been treated by some very talented medical personnel, so he can more readily assess a treatment than the average patient. He admitted that he felt better, and his spine felt stronger as well!

We continue to work on Simon as problems appear.

CHAPTER 28 – ALLERGIES & SINUSITIS

North Carolina is one of the most allergy prone states in the country. There are a great deal of mold, mildew, grasses, pollen, animals, and other irritants in this state that many people are sensitive to. Springtime, with all of its emerging vegetation, is quite difficult for many individuals. What may begin as a simple allergic reaction can quickly turn into sinusitis, eventually resulting in a painful and achy body!

Brother Harold ran into several people with sinusitis during the past year. I saw these infections appear as yellow patches while working with Brother Harold. It does not matter whether they are bacterial or viral, they all appear with the same yellow energy footprint.

When Brother Harold goes to visit a patient with sinusitis, initially he checks the patient's body for any other symptoms. Once, for example, we unexpectedly spied cancer spreading throughout the body of one patient. It appeared as black seeds which we quickly treated. After a quick body check is performed, the head is next.

As I watch Brother Harold perform his scan, I can see the head and then deeper inside, the sinuses become visible. The sinuses are drained first, which allows the mucus trapped inside to clear out. Usually, I assume the patient finds themselves quite actively blowing their nose during this process! It does take a few minutes to drain all the sinuses, and it is done rather sedately.

Once the sinuses are drained, Brother Harold showers them with treatments of yellow healing energy. Wave after wave of the energy is flooded through the sinuses, which is meant to destroy any remaining bacteria or viruses. Finally, a calming and healing energy bath works to return all the sinuses to their formerly healthy state.

Normally, a one-time treatment is all that is required to help the suffering patient. Occasionally, if the sinusitis attack is severe, a second visit might be necessary. If the patient's sinusitis has been active for a long period of time, often a repeat third or fourth visit is needed.

Quite often, chest colds have developed as a result of the constant mucus production in the sinus cavities along with its associated post nasal drainage. Brother Harold works on the lungs and bronchial airways, and will complete any necessary cleaning and healing. Smokers in particular, have often been helped as Brother Harold cleans out the tar and residue from their habit which has accumulated in their lungs.

The first time I witnessed Brother Harold's skill in this particular area, we were working on a cancer patient in Wilmington. He had complained of breathing difficulties, and felt unable to get a full breath of air. Since our patient was a smoker, we anticipated the worst. We arrived and saw both lungs completely clogged up with tar and its associated trash due to his smoking habit. Brother Harold worked carefully, and meticulously removed every bit of tarry residue that he found. He would aim his energy light at each small piece of trash he found, and reduced its size without harming the lung. This was a long

116

and tedious process, but he continued for approximately ten or fifteen minutes. Finally, we stopped and studied his lungs. They were both spotlessly clean and operating very well!

After this experience, I remembered my own smoking habit from 14 until 41 years of age and realized how nasty my own lungs probably were. When we finished in Wilmington, I asked Brother Harold to check and clear out my own lungs! I can say, from first hand experience, that I can breathe more deeply now than I ever have!

I have helped many people breathe easier simply by asking Brother Harold to clean their lungs. Admittedly, this exercise does help to turn someone into a quick believer of spirit medicine if this person had little faith in it to begin with! I learned, however, that people suffering from advanced cases of diseases which affects their breathing capability are often not fully able to appreciate the effects of cleaned out lungs.

CHAPTER 29 – PLANTAR FASCIITIS

Mary is one of the most intelligent women I know. She has a very high IQ, and is quite adept at crossword puzzles and excels in her job as well! She is a registered nurse who works in the intensive care unit of a local hospital. If I ever need critical care, I feel very relieved to know that Mary would be able to care for me.

Recently, Mary asked me to bring Brother Harold to assist her. She was feeling quite a bit of pain while walking on her left foot. Being familiar with all of her symptoms, Mary correctly assumed that she was being plagued with plantar fasciitis. A few months ago, we had treated her right foot with a similar problem. Three treatments later, it was repaired and afterwards, she had no problem walking on her foot. Now, it was time to do the same procedure on her other foot.

On our first visit to Mary's left foot, we looked it over. When Brother Harold slowed down and started studying specific areas during his exam, lights appeared on her foot. These indicated particular areas which he obviously felt needed extra attention. Perhaps he felt that the bone was positioned a little too high in each of those spots? Every highlighted area was granted two minutes of treatment, during which it received illumination with a laser-like light.

Mary had also complained about a painful outside edge on her foot. Brother Harold started to sand down its left edge. After we finished, I felt positive about the anticipated results of her treatment. Mary is a large woman who puts a lot of pressure on her feet as she walks. Due to the nature of her position, I was absolutely sure she walked quite a bit daily!

Later feedback from Mary let us know that she felt better, but was far from cured. Our second visit yielded the same results and treatment protocol. Unfortunately, Mary's feedback did not produce what we expected would be a good outcome.

After Brother Harold and I visited Mary four more times, she was feeling somewhat frustrated. I was extremely frustrated. I had a strong feeling that Brother Harold was becoming frustrated, too! This would be the first time that I would see that, or so I expected.

Again, we went back and I watched Brother Harold carefully, expecting the worst from someone who is frustrated. Surprisingly, I discovered that Brother Harold had another lesson to teach me. We returned to Mary's left foot, but this time he did not treat it. Brother Harold examined it very carefully, looking at it from every direction and every depth possible.

Unexpectedly, Brother Harold and I traveled together to Mary's left knee and slowly worked our way down. We went through all of the muscles from her knee to her ankle, and inspected everything. As we finished, we found ourselves back at her foot where we had begun. The lights which Brother Harold had placed in Mary's foot were still there, but glowed very faintly.

Suddenly, all the lights went out and I received a spirit fax from Brother Harold.

Mary's left foot has received all the treatments it should. I suggest that Mary start exercising her calf muscle for about five minutes before she starts walking on her foot in the morning.

Immediately, I apologized to Brother Harold for expecting anything less than failure from him! Without any delay, I phoned Mary and gave her his message. Two days later, Mary called me back. Her mood was ebullient!

I knew it could be nothing less than good news. Mary had followed his advice for the last two days, and she was without pain! She was not sure of her results after just one day of exercise, so she waited until it had worked for two days in a row. Mary was now a believer and she is very thankful for Brother Harold's advice!

CHAPTER 30 – FIBROMYALGIA & OTHERS

MJ had been a friend of mine for five or six years before Brother Harold and I started to work together. MJ is an enthusiastic believer in everything we have done, and has become a witness to our effectiveness.

My friend has had a very difficult life. Several years ago, MJ had been married to an alcoholic and unfortunately was the recipient of far too many regular beatings from her husband. When her husband lost his job, all of them, including their son, fell into hard times and were in danger of becoming homeless. MJ's mother invited them to live with her in her house, and they readily accepted. This arrangement continued for several years until MJ discovered that her mother and her husband were having an affair.

When MJ confronted her mother with her discovery, she readily admitted it. She was shocked when her mother then informed her that she regretted giving birth to MJ, and if she had been given the opportunity, she would have had an abortion. MJ was devastated to discover that she had been an unwanted child.

One often reads about such destructive behavior within a family, but hearing from a dear friend that she was subjected to this, makes it personal and even harder to bear. Sadly, her son grew up and developed the same destructive behavior pattern as his father. MJ is now haunted by the memories of her husband, as his liver could only take so much abuse before it ultimately failed and he passed away. Her mother is still alive and lives very close to where MJ now resides.

MJ came to me for help a year ago, and Brother Harold helped her recover from a bleeding ulcer. After her ulcer healed, she received some psychiatric therapy, and started to take prescription mood elevators. MJ was doing quite well for about five or six months, until she began to have vision problems.

Brother Harold examined her after an ophthalmologist felt that high blood pressure was affecting the vision in one of her eyes. After this information was relayed to Brother Harold, he initiated treatments which significantly improved her vision! After a few weeks of Brother Harold's treatments, she noticed that it had improved permanently. All treatments ceased and everything was going well until recently.

Suddenly, MJ began to have severe attacks of depression. They seemed to be coupled with problems which were a result of Fibromyalgia, a disease she had been diagnosed with a few years earlier. Because I remembered the two previous attacks I had experienced with this disease in previous patients, I carefully followed Brother Harold as we went to visit her. All proceeded normally until my vision suddenly went dark!

After a moment, I saw some blue energy hovering in front of me. I had no idea what this was, and quickly started calling Brother Harold. This energy did not move! Brother Harold arrived and sent a band of low energy toward it to determine what we were dealing with. His low energy band approached the blue band, and started moving all around it, poking into every area.

After thirty seconds, this strange blue energy was surrounded by Brother Harold's energy. Suddenly, our attack began with serious energy bolts shooting from Brother Harold directed at and hitting the blue energy. These bolts continued to attack and more energy was looped around this odd blue entity.

Our entire fight lasted for eight or nine minutes and in the end, the blue energy was completely destroyed. It had moved around trying to avoid the energy bolts shot at it, but had not attacked Brother Harold. When the fight was over, Dr. Price stopped any further action for the day. My energy level was getting too low for us to safely continue.

I knew that we had started to deal with MJ's current challenge. Whether we had dealt with the cause of her problems, I seriously doubted. The emotional and psychological pain inflicted on MJ by her mother and husband is incalculable. Brother Harold has not effectively treated patients with psychiatric problems so far, but as we are learning, nothing is impossible.

CHAPTER 31 – MESSAGE ON DISEASE CAUSES

I feel compelled to talk about diseases and their causes. This chapter's content comes from Brother Harold, and contains his third message to everyone.

Today, we are knowledgeable about many bacterial and viral causes for a variety of diseases. Brother Harold would like everyone to know about other causes which can be equally deadly.

Since I have been privileged enough to visit several patients with Brother Harold, it is obvious that some diseases are evil at their core. Within some illnesses, there is a darkness that overwhelms the body which prevents light from reaching parts of it. Some of these diseases have been controlled by thinking entities.

I have witnessed the mortality that controls these diseases. At times, I have witnessed Brother Harold attack and kill the invading entity and its offspring. On one occasion, this occurred during a battle in a patient with Celiac Disease. While viewing the patient's body, I saw a small living thing. It was not human, but it had blue energy, and all around it were additional tiny pieces of blue energy. Brother Harold viewed these entities for two minutes, and then attacked them until they were all dead. I am aware that bacteria and viruses are alive, but this was beyond that known form of life.

When I encounter a bacterium or a virus, it appears as a yellow entity. Likewise, when I see a human spirit which has just crossed over, it also appears as a yellow energy. Within a few days of a person's passing, I can see that the human spirit has transitioned into a blue energy. Given what I have seen and learned, I interpret the blue energy color to be connected with higher and more advanced spiritual entities.

Using this interpretation, I deduced that the blue energy witnessed in the Celiac Disease patient also appeared to be a more advanced, living entity which controlled the disease. When I think about this, I find that information frightening! Taking Two Feathers with me on our spiritual medical healing journeys has made his protection for me doubly meaningful.

Another disease factor appears to involve its age within the patient. I worked on two women, both with Celiac Disease, on the same day. They were both members of the same support group, all of whom suffer from Celiac Disease. One of these ladies, who had suffered with the disease for a longer period of time, was the patient where I encountered the entities with blue energy which we battled. The other woman had no blue energy within her.

When I was with Brother Harold treating a wheelchair-bound woman from California who had suffered from Fibromyalgia for years, I experienced another life form in her body. While Brother Harold performed his work, I was looking at the muscles in the woman's body. I wondered how a muscle could be so damaged, appearing as if a small hand grenade had exploded within it. At that point, a small robot-like machine exited out of a hole in the muscle and seemed to be looking around. It looked as if it were a sophisticated machine that had been produced in Japan, and appeared to be made out of stainless steel. Of course, it had been made in the woman's body, but its intricacy was amazing.

Suddenly, that robot fired bursts of energy at me! I quickly asked Two Feathers to add more screens to protect me, and I asked him to attack. He did and was victorious.

The third and last time I have encountered other life-forms, occurred in another Fibromyalgia patient. This time a piece of muscle, similar to a piece of liver, moved slowly out of one of her muscles and started firing little energy shots at me. It was a very weak attempt from what was evidently a new life form. Its intent was obvious and Two Feathers ended another robot's life.

Three times I have encountered other life-forms, each related to an autoimmune disease. Clearly, the longer a person has the disease, the more advanced the life-form is within the body. That is a very frightening thought. Imagining the possibilities of super-advanced entities in a person who has had a disease for ten or twenty years is daunting!

I find the concept of a disease attacking the person trying to cure the disease problematic as well. This certainly raises the stakes involved in a fight considerably for a medical helper. Fighting these battles can sometimes be more dangerous than actually catching an infection from a patient.

Treating Lupus patients has also been enlightening. I personally feel that Lupus is an evil disease. It has a tendency to take over portions of the body, blocking their use by the end of the disease process. There have been times when I have wondered if the patient's general attitude toward life might play a part as a cause of an illness? Diseases that methodically advance until a system is taken over and incapacitated, engenders such ruminations.

Brother Harold left these words with me that I want to share with others.

Let all people become aware of the evil lurking within many diseases. Evil takes many forms. It can be disguised as a harmful and devastating disease, making it difficult to defeat. Sometimes this evil can be caused by a person's own attitudes towards life, especially if they are always sad or negative attitudes and feelings of lack of self worth. The greatest good we can do is to expose our negativity to sunshine and realize that we are all good, and all happens for the good of man and God. It is my prayer that the right people will read and understand this, and can take appropriate actions. May all patients so afflicted with these evil diseases come to good endings.

CHAPTER 32 – WEDNESDAY NIGHTS

Our Wednesday night Development Circle meetings continue, and they consistently start the same way each time. Normally, we open with a welcoming speech and prayer.

We welcome the spirits who come to our meeting. We ask that only the highest and best spirits are allowed to attend. All other spirits, we ask for them to return to where they came from.

We welcome all of the Native American spirits who came to this meeting – they are all welcome. We thank them for their protection, their knowledge that they share with us, and their friendship. Chief Watonga is also welcome to attend the meeting.

We welcome the many healing spirits who attend, and as they look down on us, we ask that they work on everyone in attendance, returning us all to our previous healthy state, in body, mind and spirit.

We would like to send healing to the people who are not present tonight. We state their names or think their names through our minds to you. We know that these people are receiving the healing we asked for, even as we speak. We thank you for the attention you give to these people.

Our purpose for meeting here is to communicate with our spirits, attempting to go higher than we have ever gone before, as close to God as we can get. We thank the spirits for their help and knowledge. We ask for all of this in the name of truth. Amen.

After we have started with our initial prayer and statement of our intent, we normally call on our spirit guides. Typically, the person to my right begins, and then the person to their right calls their guides. We proceed, traveling counter clockwise around the circle, before ending with myself.

Once all of our spirits have been invited, the meeting begins. This is an open meeting and anyone may speak, in any order. There may be quiet for long periods of time, as each person usually communicates with their own spirits silently. If anyone sees anything of value, experiences anything of interest, or receives a message for anyone, they simply start to talk.

In recent meetings, we have experienced the arrival of one or more angels. On one particular occasion, a large male angel appeared, standing on the table in the middle of the room. He carried a rolled piece of paper, which he would unroll and from which he would read, saying a prayer. Intuitively, I feel that he is new at this particular task, being escorted by other, more experienced angels. I always thank all of the angels for their presence and participation in our meeting. Their presence is always appreciated by all of the circle attendees.

My mother appears every Wednesday, and she carries with her a light that shines with a variety of colors, which she will turn on or off, as she sees fit. The Circle and I are still puzzling out the meaning of
132

this light, and its different colors. Her attendance is valued, and her obvious willingness to help any member of the group is appreciated. She frequently comforts anyone who is ill, or suffering through the loss of a loved one. She has always been there for us, and I see this as symbolic and a reflection of her long ago nursing and healing skills.

There are a few "Joy Guides" that visit our group as well. These are young and cheerful spirits whose main pursuit is to bring joy and laughter to people. One of our members, Lou, has a Leprechaun named Jimmy who likes to dress up in various costumes, and enjoys pestering Daisy, a young girl who is my wife's Joy Guide. One Wednesday, Jimmy appeared dressed as a clown and Daisy showed up wearing a pumpkin head! They proceeded to parade gleefully around the room so that each person could appreciate what they looked like.

After an hour of messages from our spirits, the meeting is completed with a final prayer.

We thank all of the spirits for their assistance during this evening's meeting. We especially thank the healing spirit for all that they do. It is greatly appreciated.

We thank the angels for their attendance and their prayers. We know as we go through the remainder of the week that we will be better able to provide guidance and leadership as a result of tonight's meeting.

We thank everyone in the name of truth. Amen.

CHAPTER 33 – THE ENDING

Every Sunday morning, Brother Harold has led me to watch a Mass on television. This particular show televises the Mass celebrated at the historic church of Notre Dame University. This year in 2006, I saw that the Easter celebration service was very well attended, and I felt Brother Harold's presence with me at the start of the service. Five minutes into the service, I could feel the intense joy that was flowing out of Brother Harold. It was a pure and wonderful joy that a devout monk would feel for the resurrection of Jesus Christ, and what it meant to all humanity.

For the first time on an Easter morning, I wept. I wept with joy as I shared the celebration of Christ's resurrection with Brother Harold. I will always remember this Easter.

I asked Brother Harold to help me end this account of our first year together. He has talked about the circularity of life, and how similar endings are to beginnings.

He asks me to remind everyone of his first message, the one reassuring us that God created all of us and to share in the joy of our spirits. We are all spirits who are given a life on earth, and we should rejoice in this in both our spirit and life. When our life on earth has ended, we will all continue on as spirits and that spiritual life continues for eternity. We should all remember these facts and celebrate them all.

I reflect back on this past year and I am reminded of the good fortune I have had and have shared with many people. Every morning when I begin my day with Brother Harold, I am grateful for my good fortune. I look forward to what I learn every day. Each person is different, and every illness requires a unique treatment. Brother Harold continues to surprise me with the inventions that exist in the spirit world, and his skillful use of them. "The simplest solution is always the best" is now a law in my world. I had always suspected that natural laws were often in play, and Brother Harold has proved me to be correct.

Still, I wonder about auto-immune diseases and their causes. Certainly, the anger we hold inside of us is one of the reasons that diseases can take hold. My wish is that anger in the world would be shed along with our ego, then the planet would be a much better place for us all!

The Development Circle continues to meet weekly, and I consider this group to be one of the biggest blessings in my life. This year, I believe that we have all developed spiritually in a dramatic way. The continual arrival and participation of new spirits and angels in our group is both comforting and invigorating. Brother Harold has been accepted as a weekly member of the group, and I appreciate the blessings he gives us.

The ongoing Native American presence in the group is also cherished. The recent appearance of Chief Watonga in our group signals the closeness between our peoples, of different races, and I celebrate his arrival. He always brings his lit peace pipe, and is often offering to share it with member after member of the group. He is always at ease around us and can usually be found seated nearby, watching the group and everything that is going on.

Looking forward, I am feeling more knowledge shared by Brother Harold with me. I expressed an interest in the machinery used on Hillary to purify her blood, which removed the candidia from her system. Immediately, I started receiving "spirit faxes", showing me how the machine was developed, various parts and some things to be careful of when developing the machine, and additional other information. Brother Harold does answer questions quite thoroughly! I appreciated his answers and the time he took to relay them to me. I eagerly look forward to all the things I know I will learn this coming year.

Today, I feel more centered than I ever have in my life. I am aware of my duties with Brother Harold. I am more in tune with the time and effort he undertakes while performing various healing tasks. I can anticipate the need to repeat visits to complete a variety of tasks, such as the setting of a disc in a spine and the need to return to verify its placement, or Brother Harold's use of medicated tape on misplaced discs in a spine of an active person.

Year one has ended. Year two has begun and new surprises have already occurred! I wanted to add to this book, but have already started the next book and have finished two chapters. I have also decided to use the summation of all I have learned the first year as a good start for year two. Already, we are treating our first medical doctor as a patient. He was given two years to live with no known treatment available on this planet. His tale excites me and I know it will excite you in my future sagas.

Life continues to be a joy for myself and Brother Harold!

THE END